THE EXECUTION
OF
ISAAC HAYNE

Isaac Hayne

THE EXECUTION

of ISAAC HAYNE

by David K. Bowden

THE SANDLAPPER STORE, INC.

Copyright ©1977 by The Sandlapper Store, Inc.
P.O. Box 841, Lexington, S.C. 29072

FIRST EDITION

Library of Congress Catalog Card Number: 76-20850
International Standard Book Number: 0-87844-037-2
Manufactured in the United States of America

To Sandy and David, Jr.

Contents

List of Illustrations 9

Foreword 11

Preface 13

I.   Life on the Pon Pon 15

II. Capture and Execution 25

III. Implications and Aftereffects 47

IV. Epilogue: Patriot and Martyr 67

     Appendix I 79

     Appendix II 83

Bibliography 87

Index 99

List of Illustrations

Frontispiece (Isaac Hayne) 2
   From Margaret Hayne Harrison: *A Charleston Album*, William
   L. Bauhan, Publisher, Dublin, N.H. (formerly Richard R. Smith,
   Rindge, N.H.)

Hayne Family Coat of Arms 17

Lord Francis Rawdon-Hastings 19

Colonel Isaac Hayne Being Led to His Execution 33

Major John André 37

Nathanael Greene 48

Lord Charles Cornwallis 55

Robert Y. Hayne 68

Paul Hamilton Hayne 69

Isaac W. Hayne 69

Monument to Colonel Isaac Hayne 73

Foreword

Publication of this account of the death of Isaac Hayne in the American Revolution is, I think, a particularly useful and appropriate way to celebrate the Bicentennial. Condemned to death by British authorities during the occupation of Charlestown in 1781, Hayne became perhaps the most prominent American to be executed during the war for treason against the Crown. Ambiguous and extenuating circumstances surrounding his conduct, the importance of his example, and his courage in facing death immediately made his case controversial and his name famous. The American commander in the South, General Nathanael Greene, threatened retaliation; after the victory at Yorktown, the Continental Congress considered a motion to take vengeance on their most important prisoner, Lord Cornwallis; while the debate over the Hayne affair in the British House of Lords almost led to a duel between an outraged Duke of Richmond and one of the men responsible for the execution. Although none of these potentially unfortunate consequences ensued, Hayne soon became a martyr celebrated in song and story. Antebellum South Carolinians, especially, discovered in him a source of inspiration and pride. Sectional strife in the nineteenth century therefore helped to insure that, having become part of the local folklore for some Americans, he would also become part of the forgotten past for others. Rescuing him from both fates may well prove to be David Bowden's special contribution in this account.

Drawing upon a wider range of sources than those used by earlier historians, Bowden examines not only the episode itself but also its context. As a result, his study transcends the limitations of its predecessors: Instead of an indictment of British "tyranny," Bowden provides an understanding of misguided policy; rather than a eulogistic tribute to Hayne's heroism, he offers an analysis of political ramifications of the entire incident. Although this approach at first appears somewhat abstract, the ultimate result is a poignant picture of an honorable man, caught up in forces beyond his control, trying to reconcile the conflicting demands of personal honor, duty to country and love for his family. That he failed and died in the attempt tells us much about the American Revolution that myth has omitted and men forgotten. For Hayne was but one of many whose names, even, are now probably lost forever. Thus his story must stand for theirs. And for their sake, as well as for his — but most of all for our own — he is worth recalling in this two hundredth year of American independence.

Department of History
University of South Carolina   Robert M. Weir

Preface

Had British authorities executed Isaac Hayne early in the Revolution, rather than on August 4, 1781, he might now be remembered as a patriot martyr of Nathan Hale's stature. Certainly the contemporary furor over each was comparable. In part because Hayne was sufficiently prominent among the planter elite to be a colonel of South Carolina militia and in part because extenuating circumstances mitigated his offense, many Americans regarded his execution as the brutal and senseless act of Colonel Nisbet Balfour and Francis, Lord Rawdon, who commanded British forces in the area.

Cries for retaliation followed Hayne's death; yet, no British officer was to suffer his fate. No doubt, contemporaries were correct in believing that the approaching end of the war deterred American authorities from seeking retribution, and their joy over the victory at Yorktown obviously tended to make them forget their wrath at Hayne's death. But the story of the immediate and long-range reaction — in both Great Britain and America — has never been fully told, and some intriguing questions about purposes realized and intentions gone awry remain to be answered.

The task of responding to these questions was made more pleasant under the perceptive guidance of Dr. Robert M. Weir. I am also grateful to Dr. George C. Rogers, Jr., for his helpful suggestions and to Miss Wylma Wates for sharing her interest in Isaac Hayne. The many courtesies extended by the staffs of the South Carolina Department of Archives and History and of the South Caroliniana Library are greatly appreciated.

13

Mr. Isaac Hayne, who since the capitulation of Charlestown; had taken protection, and acknowledged himself a subject of his Majesty's Government, having notwithstanding been taken in arms, and at the head of a Rebel Regiment of Militia, was therefore on Saturday morning last, executed as a Traitor.

Royal Gazette
Charlestown
August 8, 1781

Chapter One
Life on the Pon Pon

The execution of Isaac Hayne caused more bitterness and raised more cries for revenge than any other single act of the British army of occupation in South Carolina during the Revolution. To understand the implications of Hayne's death, it will first be helpful to understand who Isaac Hayne was and why the death of this particular man caused such extreme public reaction.

Hayne, the son of Isaac Hayne and Sarah Williamson and grandson of John Hayne and Mary Deane, was born September 23, 1745. The elder Isaac had been born July 27, 1714, and died on December 23, 1751. John Hayne, the progenitor of the Hayne family in South Carolina, settled in Colleton County in 1700 and appears to have come from Shropshire, England. The elder Isaac was first a deacon and then an elder of the Bethel Presbyterian Church and Congregation of Pon Pon, St. Bartholomew's Parish, Colleton.[1] A respected member of the community, in 1748 Isaac was elected to the Seventeenth Royal Assembly as a representative from St. Bartholomew's Parish; but he declined to serve.[2] In 1751 he was appointed commissioner to build a new bridge over the Pon Pon River. He was also one of the petit jurors and grand jurors for St. Bartholomew's parish.[3] After his death in 1751, his estate was inventoried and valued at nearly £19,000 South Carolina currency.[4]

On July 18, 1765, the younger Isaac married Elizabeth Hutson, the daughter of the Reverend William Hutson, pastor of Stoney Creek and later of the Independent Church in Charlestown. Isaac

15

and Elizabeth had seven children: Isaac, born July 2, 1766; Mary, born April 11, 1768; Sarah, born August 10, 1770; John, born February 8, 1773; Elizabeth, born November 17, 1774; Mary, born August 29, 1776; and William Edward, born August 29, 1776.[5]

As his father had been before him, Isaac Hayne was elected to represent St. Bartholomew's Parish. Isaac replaced James Reid in the Twenty-Ninth Royal Assembly and qualified on February 2, 1770. In 1770 he was elected commissioner for stamping and issuing money to defray the expense of building courthouses and jails.[6] In 1777 he was elected to the Second General Assembly for St. Paul's Parish, but he declined to serve. His name appeared on the petit jury and grand jury lists for St. Bartholomew's in 1778. He was later elected to the Third General Assembly and served in the Senate during 1779 and 1780 for the parish of St. Bartholomew.[7]

At the time of the Revolution, Hayne was enjoying a profitable plantation life. Hayne Hall, located four miles from Jacksonborough, was an "elegant mansion house — brick barn, and stables, and every suitable building of a well settled rice plantation."[8] This plantation was Hayne's residence and contained about nine hundred acres. Hayne's holdings included two other plantations called Pear Hill and Sycamore which had seven hundred and six hundred and fifty acres, respectively. He owned five lots in Beaufort and two lots in Charlestown, plus an additional 6,377 acres, most of which was in the Up Country. He also owned one thousand acres in Georgia and some land in the New Acquisition.[9] In York District he was a partner with William Hill in the Aera Ironworks that manufactured ammunition for the use of the American forces.[10] According to his cousin, Robert Y. Hayne, Hayne was well-educated and highly respected in the community and was a breeder of fine horses.[11] His efficiency is attested to in the way he meticulously recorded the births, deaths and marriages that he knew of in the Low Country and kept his own plantation notes.[12]

The war was soon to interrupt Hayne's comfortable plantation life. In January of 1776, Hayne, a captain in the militia, went to Charlestown with one hundred and sixty privates and thirteen officers who had last been posted at Dorchester.[13] After his return to Hayne Hall, his brother-in-law, Richard Hutson, kept him informed of military activity in and around Charlestown. Ironically

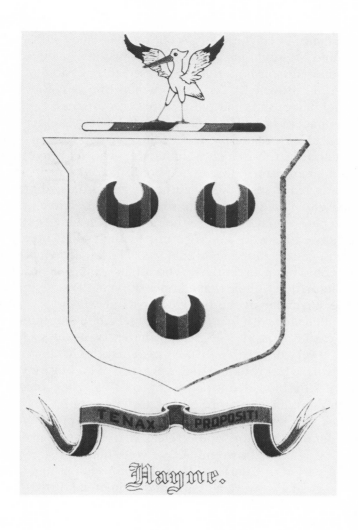

The coat of arms borne by the Hayne family of South Carolina.

in June of that year Hutson wrote about the man who would be a decisive factor in Hayne's fate. A cocked hat laced with gold had been found off Simmons Island. Lord Rawdon's name was in the crown, and Hutson hopefully expressed the possibility that the "villain" had drowned.[14] As Hayne would find out, Rawdon was very much alive; and their paths were soon to cross.

The impact of Isaac Hayne's death can be better understood by looking at the events of the preceeding year. In May of 1780, Sir Henry Clinton, the British commander who had invested and captured Charlestown, threatened confiscation of property of all who continued to resist Royal authority and promised protection to those who would support the British. He proclaimed that prisoners on parole could return to their homes. On June 1 full pardon was promised all who would return to their allegiance, except those who had executed loyal subjects. Clinton had feared at first that he could not protect those who might want to be loyal to the king. Clinton determined that all opposition in the state had ended with the surrender of the outlying posts at Ninety Six, Augusta and Camden, and with Lieutenant Colonel Abraham Buford's men at the Waxhaws on May 29. Since Charlestown was secured and offered "a very defensible fortress as an asylum for the friends of government to resort to and they were sure of finding most perfect security," Clinton called for a return to British allegiance.[15]

While the inhabitants of South Carolina were on parole, they could not hurt or, more important, could not support the British effort. Clinton then on June 3 released from their paroles as of June 20 all "who had surrendered or were taken prisoners before the capitulation of Charlestown (excepting such as had served in the military line or were actually in confinement at the taking of that town and Fort Moultrie)," and proclaimed as rebels all who would not take an oath of allegiance to the king.[16] This proclamation was an ultimatum to those on parole, and many who would have happily remained neutral were forced to choose sides in the war.[17]

Various accounts are given of Isaac Hayne's role during and after the siege of Charlestown. Apparently he served in the Colleton County Regiment of militia behind the British lines and was

Painting by Sir Joshua Reynolds, courtesy South Caroliniana Library

Francis Rawdon-Hastings (1754-1826), called by the historian Fortesque "the ablest of all" the British officers in the American Revolution, commanded British forces in South Carolina after Cornwallis and was a principal figure in Hayne's death. Lord Rawdon overcame an attempt at public censure for his participation and later, after he had become the Earl of Moira, had a distinguished military career in India.

not in the city at its surrender. One version said that Hayne retired two hundred miles into the backcountry where he was captured and taken to Charlestown. There he took protection rather than be put on a prison ship.[18] Another source recounted that Hayne voluntarily surrendered with the hope that he would be paroled to his plantation. He found, however, that "he must either become a British subject, or submit to close confinement."[19] A third story stated that Hayne was covered under the Articles of Capitulation, and, therefore, returned to his home on parole. Hayne's neighbor, Colonel Robert Ballingall, a Royal militia officer for their district, summoned him to come to Charlestown as a prisoner or to swear allegiance to the Crown. Hayne then signed an agreement to act as a British subject as long as the British controlled the area.[20]

All the accounts agreed that Hayne ended up in Charlestown where he took an oath. At that time Hayne's wife and children were gravely ill with smallpox.[21] Hayne said that the "deplorable Situation of his Family, his Wife & Children then being dangerously ill, & the Country wasted, had compelled him, for saving their Lives, to come to Chas. Town, to get a Physician, & procure Necessaries for the sick."[22] When James Simpson, the intendant of the Board of Police, and Brigadier General James Patterson, the first commandant of Charlestown, demanded that Hayne remain in Charlestown or sign an oath of allegiance, Hayne chose the latter.[23] Hayne later stated "that he wd. submit to their government, & take the *oath*, but, must openly declare, that he shd. consider it as obligatory, only as long as their Protection wd. really be of Benefit to him, or, till the Americans wd. again get possession of the Country."[24]

Governor Rutledge confirmed that Hayne had made a declaration of allegiance rather than an oath to the commandant of Charlestown and that James Simpson, on behalf of the commandant, had "assured him that it was not expected that he shd. bear Arms against the Americans, nor adhere to the Allegiance which he promised, any longer than he shd. receive Protection."[25] Patterson and Simpson further added "that when the regular forces could not defend the country without the aid of its inhabitants, it would be high time for the Royal army to quit it."[26] The British, however, were not able to keep their promise of protection.

Footnotes, Chapter I

[1] Theodore D. Jervey, "The Hayne Family," *South Carolina Historical and Genealogical Magazine,* V (July, 1904), 168-188; George Howe, *History of the Presbyterian Church in South Carolina,* (Columbia: Duffie and Chapman, 1870), I, 475-479.

[2] Joan Schreiner Reynolds Faunt, Robert E. Rector and David K. Bowden, comps., *Biographical Directory of the South Carolina House of Representatives,* Walter B. Edgar, ed., (Columbia: University of South Carolina Press, 1974), I, 98.

[3] Thomas Cooper and David J. McCord, *The Statutes at Large of South Carolina,* (Columbia: A. S. Johnston, 1838-1841), IX, 156-159; Jury and Tax Lists, Box II, 1751-1779, South Carolina Department of Archives and History.

[4] The elder Isaac Hayne's estate was inventoried on March 17, 1752, and the total estate value was set at £18,808 19/3^d. He had fifty-two slaves valued at £10,800, one hundred head of cattle at £400, twenty-five horses at £562, and fifty sheep at £100, and three hundred bushels of rough rice at £150 in addition to corn, peas, sundry books, tools, pewterware, silverware, furniture and miscellaneous household goods. He also had one hundred forty-five barrels of clean rice worth £1450 in addition to sundry bonds, notes and cash on hand valued at £3099. Charleston County Inventories Microfilm, 1751-1753, South Carolina Department of Archives and History. Wallace lists the value of South Carolina currency for the year 1749 as 700-725 currency equals £100. David Duncan Wallace, *South Carolina: A Short History, 1520-1948,* (Columbia: University of South Carolina Press, 1951), p. 136.

[5] Jervey, *South Carolina Historical and Genealogical Magazine,* V, 180-181.

[6] Cooper and McCord, *Statutes of South Carolina,* IV, 323-325; Faunt, Rector and Bowden, *Biographical Directory of the S. C. House of Representatives,* I, 137.

[7] Faunt, Rector and Bowden, *Biographical Directory of the S. C. House of Representatives,* I, 175; Jury and Tax Lists, Box II, 1751-1779, South Carolina Department of Archives and History. Emily Bellinger Reynolds and Joan

Reynolds Faunt, *Biographical Directory of the Senate of the State of South Carolina, 1776-1964,* (Columbia: South Carolina Department of Archives and History, 1964), p. 17. A possible explanation of why Hayne declined to serve is found in a letter from his brother-in-law, Richard Hutson, to him written January 18, 1777: "I think it will be extraordinary if I should give you the first intelligence of your election as a Representative in Assembly for the Parish of St. Paul, Stono. It will indeed convince me that you are a recluse. The return was made to the House on Wednesday last. It is said that you had but four votes, and it has been thrown out by some of the high churchmen that were they in your situation they would not serve, but I hope you will make it a point at this juncture, as we stand in need of your assistance." Edward McCrady, *The History of South Carolina in the Revolution, 1775-1780,* (New York: MacMillan Co., 1901), pp. 212-213.

[8] William Edward Hayne to Jeremiah A. Yates, Charleston, December 23, 1835, William Edward Hayne Manuscript, South Caroliniana Library.

[9] In Hayne's will, proved March 15, 1783, he divided his property among his children. He also left "Shares in the Charles town Library Society & Insurance Company & my Books and Manuscripts." He asked that "no Cost be spared in the Children's Education." Charleston County Wills, XX (1783-1786), South Carolina Department of Archives and History, 46-49.

[10] The first ironworks in South Carolina, Aera Furnace, was twenty-two feet square and was built by Hill and subsidized by £7,000 from the state. Hayne provided the labor force to build and work the foundry. Profits were equally shared by Hayne and Hill. Tories destroyed the ironworks and carried off ninety slaves in 1780. Hill and Hayne Aera and Aetna Ironworks, 1798-1802, and Sheriff's Records of William E. Hayne, York District, 1809-1815, York County Records Microfilm, South Carolina Department of Archives and History; Articles of Co-Partnership between Isaac Hayne and William Hill concerning Aera Ironworks, March 3, 1778, Subject File (Iron Industry), South Carolina Department of Archives and History. An advertisement offered "by wholesale or retail, bar and plow share iron, Smith's and forge anvils and hammers, pots of all sizes, kettles both for kitchen and camp, skillets, Dutch ovens,...spice mortars, waggon, cart and truck boxes, salt pans, stoves, andirons, swivel guns...or any other kind of casting in iron." *South Carolina and American General Gazette* (Charlestown), December 3, 1779.

[11] Robert Y. Hayne, "The Execution of Colonel Isaac Hayne," *Southern Review,* I (1828), 75-76.

[12] "Records Kept by Colonel Isaac Hayne," *South Carolina Historical and Genealogical Magazine,* X (July, 1909), 145-170, and (October 1909), 220-235; XI (January, 1910), 27-38, (April, 1910), 92-106, and (July, 1910), 160-170; and XII (January, 1911), 14-23.

[13] "Journal of the Council of Safety," *Collections of the South Carolina Historical Society,* (Charleston: South Carolina Historical Society, 1859), III, 184.

[14] Hutson states, "One day the week before last, a hat was taken up off of Simmons's Island by some persons going in a boat to town, and carried to the President. It was cocked Jockey fashion, laced with gold, had a cockade and feather in it, and on the inside of the crown Lord Rawden's name in Capitals. This is the villain that was coming out a volunteer against America. By the President's orders Capt. Ladson with a detachment of his company went down to Simmons's Island to search the Beach, where they found the Quarter-Galleries, and several other parts of a large new ship also two new large flat-bottomed boats one of which is capable of carrying Thirty Barrels of Rice and the other five and twenty. So that in all probability Lord Rawden has met with a fate which I think he merited for voluntarily engaging in such nefarious service." "Letters of the Hon. Richard Hutson," *Charleston Yearbook.* (1895), pp. 313-325.

[15] William B. Willcox, ed., *The American Rebellion: Sir Henry Clinton's Narrative of His Campaigns, 1775-1782, with an Appendix of Original Documents.* (New Haven: Yale University Press, 1954), p. 174.

[16] Willcox, ed., *The American Rebellion.* p. 181; Wallace, *South Carolina: A Short History. 1520-1948.* p. 296; Franklin and Mary Wickwire, *Cornwallis: The American Adventure.* (Boston: Houghton Mifflin Co., 1970), pp. 182-183; and George Smith McCowen, Jr., *The British Occupation of Charleston, 1780-82.* (Columbia: University of South Carolina Press, 1972), pp. 66-67.

[17] Clinton said about his June 3 proclamation: "This I looked upon as a most prudent measure, because under the sanction of those paroles a great number of inveterate rebels might remain in the country, and by their underhand and secret counsel and other machinations prevent the return of many well disposed persons to their allegiance, and [in] other ways retard the restoration of tranquillity and order. But by thus obliging every man to declare and evince his principles I gave the loyalists an opportunity of detecting and chasing from among them such dangerous neighbors, which they could not with any propriety have attempted as long as those paroles continued in force and the persons sanctioned by them were not guilty of an open breach of their promise." Willcox, ed., *The American Rebellion,* p. 181.

[18] Cover Letter to Hayne Papers, Papers of the Continental Congress, 1774-1789, no. 155, II, 349-350, National Archives Microfilm, South Carolina Department of Archives and History.

[19] David Ramsay, *The History of the Revolution of South Carolina From a British Province to an Independent State.* (Trenton: Isaac Collins, 1785), II, 277-280.

[20] In the Revolution Hayne had served first as a captain in the Colleton militia; then, when a junior officer was placed over him, he resigned his commission and enlisted as a private. Edward McCrady, *The History of South Carolina in the Revolution, 1780-1783.* (New York: MacMillan Co., 1902), pp. 130-134; Henry Lee, *Memoirs of the War in the Southern Department of the United States,* (New York: University Publishing Co., 1869), pp. 449-451.

[21] Robert Y. Hayne gave a very sympathetic picture of Hayne during this period. Prisoners on parole as Hayne was at that time were supposed to be protected but were instead the victims of plundered estates. Prisoners could not dispose of their property, follow any profession or be employed for labor. The "wretched and starving American [was] compelled to seek bread for himself and his children" by swearing allegiance to the king. The families of any men who did not profess allegiance to England were ordered to leave Charlestown. Hayne's oath of allegiance came because of these circumstances and the illness of his wife and children who "lay at the point of death." Robert Y. Hayne, "The Execution of Colonel Isaac Hayne," *Southern Review, I* (1828), 81. Isaac's son William Edward, who was five years old at the time of his father's death, recalled the event in a letter written in 1835. He confirmed that his mother died with smallpox in August of 1780. Two children died about the same time: Eliza, eighteen months old, and Mary, four years old. William was so ill that a coffin was prepared for him. William Edward Hayne Manuscript, South Caroliniana Library. Lee, *Memoirs of the War,* pp. 450-451; McCrady, *The History of South Carolina in the Revolution, 1780-1783,* p. 133.

[22] John Rutledge to John Dickinson, Letters Relating to Isaac Hayne, Manuscript Collection, Library Company of Philadelphia.

[23] Lorenzo Sabine, *Biographical Sketches of Loyalists of the American Revolution,* (Boston: Little, Brown and Co., 1864), II, 304; McCowen, *The British Occupation of Charleston, 1780-82,* p. 16. Ramsay, *The History of the Revolution of South Carolina,* II, 278-279.

[24] John Rutledge to John Dickinson, Letters Relating to Isaac Hayne, Manuscript Collection, Library Company of Philadelphia.

[25] John Rutledge to John Dickinson, Letters Relating to Isaac Hayne, Manuscript Collection, Library Company of Philadelphia.

[26] Ramsay, *The History of the Revolution of South Carolina,* II, 280.

Chapter Two
Capture and Execution

The British had controlled Charlestown since Major General Benjamin Lincoln's capitulation in May of 1780. On August 16, General Horatio Gates, newly appointed commander of the Southern Department, was defeated at Camden by Lord Cornwallis, who had been left in command of British forces in the South after Clinton returned to New York. This victory heightened the prospects of British success in the South. Two days later Banastre Tarleton followed up Cornwallis' victory with a surprise attack on General Thomas Sumter at Fishing Creek.

These two victories encouraged Cornwallis to try his luck in North Carolina. He made plans to proceed to Charlotte in September and ordered Major Patrick Ferguson, who commanded a group of Loyalists in western South Carolina, to move north toward Charlotte also. Ferguson's trip was interrupted by his overwhelming defeat at King's Mountain on October 7. This loss shattered Cornwallis' plans and he withdrew from Charlotte back to Winnsborough.

Gates was relieved of his command in the South and Nathanael Greene was named his successor, officially assuming command on December 2, 1780. Greene promptly divided his army and sent Daniel Morgan to the western part of the state, while he took the rest of his force and moved to Cheraw. Cornwallis then acted by sending Tarleton in pursuit of Morgan. Unfortunately for the

British, Tarleton caught Morgan at the Cowpens on January 17, 1781, and suffered a humiliating defeat.

Cornwallis pushed north to try and keep Morgan from reuniting with Greene and, although he failed to do so, he chased them across North Carolina and into Virginia. Greene did not stay in Virginia, however, and finally met Cornwallis at the Battle of Guilford Courthouse in North Carolina on March 15. Although Greene retreated and left Cornwallis holding the field, the British commander, still a long way from his supply base, at first proceeded to Wilmington, then continued to Virginia, never to return to South Carolina. Greene, however, turned back to Camden to join Francis Marion and Henry Lee and to deal with Lieutenant Colonel Lord Rawdon, whom Cornwallis had left in command of the post at Camden and of the South Carolina frontier. Rawdon was warned of the approach of Greene and on April 25 attacked him at Hobkirk's Hill before Marion and Lee could reinforce the Continentals.[1]

Sir Henry Clinton—alerted by a letter from Colonel Nisbet Balfour, the commandant of Charlestown—was apprehensive about Cornwallis' decision to go to North Carolina, leaving Rawdon in a dangerous situation. Indeed, the month of May brought serious setbacks for the British in 1781. Although Greene was defeated at Hobkirk's Hill, he had the advantage over Rawdon who, isolated from food and forage by the activity of partisan bands, was preparing to evacuate Camden. In May Rawdon went to Monck's Corner. In addition to problems of supplies, he had to contend with the fears of his men, many of whom were American deserters, that they might share the fate of the captives of Hobkirk's Hill who were hanged by the Americans as traitors.[2]

Balfour met Rawdon and told him of the serious situation in Charlestown. Balfour contended that "the revolt was universal," that the old fortifications in Charlestown had been leveled and that the new ones were not ready, and that the townspeople were defecting.[3] On May 11 Sumter captured Orangeburg, while Marion took Fort Motte on May 12; and three days later Lee took Fort Granby. Lee and General Andrew Pickens then marched to the Savannah and besieged Augusta on May 22.

On May 24 from Monck's Corner, Rawdon and Balfour issued a proclamation urging the people of South Carolina to remain loyal to the king: "Although attention to the general security of the province has obliged his majesty's troops, for the present, to relinquish some of the upper parts of it, we trust, that it is unnecessary for us to exhort the loyal inhabitants of those districts to stand firm in their duty and principles; or to caution them against the insidious artifices of an enemy, who must shortly abandon to their fate, those unfortunate people whom they have deluded into revolt." The proclamation further assured them that British reinforcements were coming shortly and that their property would be returned.[4] However, the British reversals were to continue.

At the time Greene, later joined by Lee and Pickens, besieged Ninety Six, where Lieutenant Colonel J. Harris Cruger had been cut off by Rawdon's withdrawal. Rawdon arrived with reinforcements from Ireland on June 21, but Greene had withdrawn the previous evening.[5] On June 20 Georgetown fell to Marion.[6]

On July 3 Cruger was ordered to evacuate Ninety Six. Again, though tactically defeated, Greene had won his strategic objective. Greene retired with his men to the High Hills of Santee for the summer.[7] From Ninety Six Rawdon had gone to Friday's Ferry to meet Lieutenant Colonel Alexander Stewart. The men, dressed in wool clothing, suffered from extreme heat, excessive marching and lack of food. Fifty men died on the march of sunstroke and exhaustion. Stewart had been called back to Charlestown so Rawdon headed for Orangeburg, where Stewart later joined him as did Cruger. Rawdon, still in ill health, gave Stewart command and left for Charlestown to sail to England.[8]

The Patriot militia of Marion, Sumter and Pickens had seemed the only threat to the British a few months earlier. However, by the spring of 1781 Balfour wrote Cornwallis, "The Defection of the Militia is also almost universal *and they have* joined the Enemy *wherever* they have come, *those to the Southward are the Worst*: one Haring [Colonel William Harden] leads the Enemy in that quarter and has over run *all the country to the Southward* of Dorchester *with a very few men*."[9] In May Balfour informed Clinton that he feared for the safety of Charlestown itself since Greene's arrival in the South:

I must inform Your Excellency that the general state of the country is most distressing [and] that the enemy's parties are everywhere. The communication by land with Savannah no longer exists; Colonel Brown is invested in Augusta, and Colonel Cruger in the most critical situation at Ninety-Six. Indeed, I should betray the duty I owe Your Excellency did I not represent the Defection of this province [as] so universal that I know of no mode short of depopulation to retain it.[10]

Reasons for these defeats for the British were, of course, many, ranging from the initial mistakes in London in sanctioning the campaign—and the failure to support it sufficiently—to the problems of distance and terrain and miscalculations of British field leaders. Of particular concern to the British was the failure of the Loyalists to turn out in the number expected. The situation in South Carolina had deteriorated, and the people who had gone over to the British for protection began to join the Americans again.[11] To reverse this trend, Clinton issued a proclamation on May 7, 1781, encouraging "Rebels or those serving in Rebel army or militia" to enlist in the British army. For a three-year enlistment, the British promised the recruit the regiment of his choice, six guineas and a grant of land.[12]

Clinton presented to Lord George Germain the picture of South Carolina in the summer of 1781. Clinton lamented that the speedy reduction of the southern provinces was not in sight. "Many untoward incidents. . .have thrown us too far back to be able to recover very soon even what we have lately lost there. For, if as I have often before suggested the good will of the inhabitants is absolutely requisite to retain a country after we have conquered it, I fear it will be some time before we can recover the confidence of those in Carolina, as their past sufferings will of course make them cautious of forwarding the King's interests before there is the strongest certainty of his army being in condition to support them."[13]

Harden had been trying to get Hayne to support the American cause, writing Marion on April 7 that Hayne had returned his commission and that his "staying on too much formality" with his oath had kept many men in the area from joining the militia. Harden added that commissions or proclamations about what would happen to those who did not choose a side would induce the men in his area to join the militia: "I find the leading men very backward, which keep many thus, so hope you will send me or some other officer some proclamations or orders what to be done on this occasion. They all say they wait for your army to come this way then they will all turn out but I find too many of them are waiting for commissions—they can't turn out without."

On April 18 Harden wrote again: "The men about Pon Pon are the backwardest though; when I first went there, I learned they were all to be in arms, only waiting till they could send a man to you for Commissions, when they were to turn out. I beg you will send some immediately with your orders, it seems they wait for Col. Hayne's and he says he can't without a Commission, and is sure, if he turns out, that at least two hundred will join him, if so, I am very sure that this part of the country may be held."[14]

The successes of Greene and the militia leaders had left the British control of little territory but Charlestown. Hayne then felt his obligation to his oath ended because "allegiance due to a conqueror ceased with his expulsion from the subdued territory."[15] Hayne became a colonel in the South Carolina militia.[16] Public records show that at least by the late spring he was active in the area, as Hayne—or men under his orders—impressed provisions for use by his forces or the public.[17]

In July near Charlestown, Colonel Hayne captured General Andrew Williamson, an American who had joined the British. Balfour, fearful that Williamson might be hanged, sent men out in force and surprised and captured Hayne.[18] Balfour informed Clinton of the capture: "Major [Thomas] Fraser, with the Mounted Men of the South Carolina Rangers, was ordered to pursue, and, if possible, retake Brigadier Williamson, as it was fear'd his having reverted to British government might subject him to the worst treatment. By avoiding the main Roads, Major Fraser was enabled to surprise Col. Haynes's Comp. of Colleton County Militia, where he was informed Gen'l Williamson then was, and coming upon it suddenly, killed a Lt. Col. McLoughlan, with ten or twelve others, made Col. Haynes a Prisoner and retook Gen'l Williamson."[19]

Hayne was held in the prison of the provost, the basement of the Exchange, while Balfour corresponded with Rawdon, who later arrived in Charlestown exhausted and ill. After Rawdon had withdrawn from Ninety Six to Orangeburg, Balfour had stressed the need of making an example of Hayne to discourage other Loyalists from breaking their oaths. Rawdon agreed. Balfour was careful to follow orders and waited for Rawdon's arrival in Charlestown to decide Hayne's fate.[20] In the letter Rawdon wrote Cornwallis on August 2, 1781, two days before the execution, he—either by intention or oversight—did not mention the Hayne affair.

The rest of Hayne's story is told through the notes he left. On July 26 Hayne received a note stating: "Sir: I am charged by the commandant to inform you that a council of general officers will assemble tomorrow at ten o'clock, in the hall of the Province, to try you." The note was from the town major, Major Charles Fraser. Later the same day Hayne received another note from Fraser stating: "Sir: I am ordered by the commandant to acquaint you that instead of a council of general officers, as is mentioned in my letter of this morning, a court of inquiry, composed of four general officers and four captains, will be assembled tomorrow at ten o'clock in the province hall, *for the purpose of determining under what point of view you ought to be considered.*"[21]

McCrady points out that the wording in the second note uses the same form of investigation that had been used in the André affair. Indeed in his 1813 letter Rawdon compared the use of a court of inquiry to its use in Major John André's case.[22] The board, of which Greene was president, had been ordered "to report a precise state of his case, and *to determine in what character he was to be considered,* and to what punishment he was liable."[23]

Hayne's account of the proceedings is in the letter of protest he later wrote Rawdon and Balfour:

> ...Having never entertained any other idea of a Court of Enquiry, nor heard of any other being formed of it, than of its serving merely to precede a council of war or some other tribunal for examining the circumstances more fully, excepting in the case of a spy, and Mr. Jarvis, lieutenant marshal to the Provost, not having succeeded in finding the person whom I named for my council, I did not take the pains to summon any witnesses, though it would have been in my power to have pro-

duced many; and I presented myself before the council without any assistance whatever. When I was before that assembly I was further convinced that I had not been deceived in my conjectures; and I found that the members of it were not sworn nor the witnesses examined on oath, and all the members as well as every person present might easily have perceived by the questions which I asked and by the whole tenor of my conduct that I had not the least notion that I was tried or examined upon an affair in which my life or death depended.[24]

The following day Rawdon and Balfour issued a joint statement sentencing Hayne:

The adjutant of the town will be so good as to go to Colonel Hayne in Provost Prison and inform him that in consequence of the court of enquiry held yesterday and the preceding evening Lord Rawdon and the commandant Lieutenant Colonel Nisbet Balfour have resolved upon his execution on Tuesday the thirty-first instant at six o'clock, for having been found under arms raising a regiment to oppose the British government, though he had become a subject and had accepted the protection of that government after the reduction of Charleston.[25]

Hayne sent for his attorney, John Colcock, who denied Rawdon's or Balfour's authority to pass such a sentence. Colcock asked that the ruling be overturned because Hayne had no knowledge of the intent of the board, because no one could be sentenced without a trial except a spy, and because Hayne's guilt had not been proven. The only reaction to this from the officers in charge was the statement that his sentence was not due to a board of inquiry ruling but by virtue of the authority with which the commander-in-chief in South Carolina and the commanding officer in Charlestown were invested.[26] The decision then rested clearly with Balfour and Rawdon, and their desire was to make an example of Hayne. The question of who had the authority to make the decision by rank did not appear to be the problem that Rawdon claimed thirty years later that it had been.[27]

Hayne then asked for a respite that he might send for his children for a last farewell. This request was denied, and at one o'clock on the morning of July 31 Hayne was told that it was time to prepare for death. Hayne was informed that he would leave for his execution at five o'clock. Major Fraser returned shortly, however, with a message: "Colonel Hayne, I am to acquaint you, that in consequence of a petition signed by Governor Bull and many more, as also of your prayer of yesterday, and the humane treatment shewn by you to the British prisoners who fell into your hands, you are respited for forty-eight hours." Fraser returned to add a part of the message that he had forgotten. A condition had been made that Hayne would be immediately executed if General Greene "should offer to expostulate . . . with the commanding officer" in Hayne's favor.[28] On August 1, Hayne was granted another forty-eight hour delay.[29]

The delays were probably granted while Balfour and Rawdon considered the entreaties for Hayne's life made by the people of Charlestown.[30] Lieutenant Governor William Bull, who had replaced Simpson as head of the Board of Police, tried to intercede for him. Two prominent Loyalists, Alexander Wright and Robert William Powell, who were appointed to assist the Board of Police, circulated petitions on Hayne's behalf.[31] Sir Egerton Leigh, the attorney general, refused to plead for him, supposedly answering that he "would burn his hand off rather than do an act so injurious to the King's service."[32] When these requests and the pleas of Hayne's own children for their father's life failed, Hayne was doomed.[33]

Hayne's son William Edward visited his father the night before his death and saw "upon one side of the door of the room of his confinement a Hessian Soldier or Centinal on the [other] side a *Coffin* covered with Black Broad Cloth & lined with white." Hayne's eldest son Isaac accompanied his father to the "place of execution & after it took charge of his body and had it [conveyed] to the place of his Residence."[34]

An eyewitness account of the execution was delivered to Congress by Isaac Neufville, a fourteen-year-old boy from Charlestown. He said that Hayne "was escorted by a party of soldiers to a gallows erected without the lines of the town with his hands tied behind, and there hung up till he was dead."[35]

Colonel Isaac Hayne Being Led from the Exchange to His Execution. August 4. 1781. **This 1973 oil painting by Carroll N. Jones, Jr., is displayed in the Major William Hazzard Wigg Memorial Room of the Fireproof Building, Charleston, headquarters for the South Carolina Historical Society. The painting is also reproduced on the dust cover of this book. Permission granted for this reproduction.**

An account attributed to Hayne's lawyer, John Colcock, tells how Hayne died: "Much has been said of the manner in which many of the old Romans met Death—but I am convinced no Man, on so serious an occasion cou'd have exhibited more Heroick Fortitude & Christian Resignation, than the unfortunate Col. Hayne: His progress to the place of Execution, (on foot, by his request) was like that of any other good Christian, on his Way to the public Service—When arrived at the Gallows, he shook hands, with a few & said Farewell my Friends—The Clergyman then went with him into the Cart & after praying by him, a considerable time took his leave—The provost Master then demanded of him, some signal when he was ready, to which he replied, I am ready at any time—pull'd his own Cap over his Eyes, &—Oh!—Cetera desunt—."[36]

A contemporary of Hayne described the day: "The streets were crowded with thousands of anxious spectators.... When the city barrier was past, and the instrument of his catastrophe appeared full in view, a faithful friend by his side observed to him, 'that he hoped he would exhibit an example of the manner in which an American can die.' He answered with the utmost tranquillity, 'I will endeavor to do so.' He ascended the cart with a firm step and serene aspect. He enquired of the executioner, who was making an attempt to get the cap over his eyes, what he wanted? Upon being informed of his design, the colonel replied, 'I will save you that trouble,' and pulled it over himself. He was afterwards asked whether he wished to say anything, to which he answered, 'I will only take leave of my friends, and be ready.' He then affectionately shook hands with three gentlemen—recommended his children to their care—and gave the signal for the cart to move."[37]

A consideration of the British situation in South Carolina in 1781 leads to the conclusion that Isaac Hayne's execution was intended to discourage further violations of parole by Americans. In addition the British intended by such a strong show of authority to eliminate the harassment by the American militia of those who were honoring their paroles. For it was claimed that, when Hayne spirited him off to set an example to anyone who might wish to forsake the American cause, General Williamson was peacefully living on his plantation.[38]

When Balfour wrote Cornwallis of his fears that Charlestown was about to fall, he showed his concern at the time and his determination to take decisive action. In an effort to intimidate the populace into adherence to their oaths, Balfour issued a stern proclamation in May of 1781 warning of a "most fixed resolution of punishing, both in their persons and properties, all those, who shall be found in arms against his Majesty's Government, after having claimed and obtained their Sovereign's most gracious protection." This is probably the "political paper" written by the Charlestown printer William Charles Wells "by request of Colonel Balfour, in which he designed to show that Whigs of rank, who, after having been taken prisoners and sent to their homes on parole, appeared in arms against the Crown, were, by military usage, and the nature of the case itself, liable to the punishment of death. This, by direction of Balfour, was frequently published in the newspapers; and it is probable that it was owing to this warning, that that officer and Lord Moira thought themselves justified in executing Colonel Hayne."[39]

The personalities of the men responsible for Hayne's death influenced their decision just as the events of the preceding year did. Because Rawdon's participation in the execution was his last official act before returning to England, some contemporaries suggest that he was fleeing the source of his criticism. This suggestion is probably unfounded. He had spent a grueling summer in combat, and his previous record reveals no neglect of duty on his part. Although he was then only twenty-six, he was an able soldier.[40] In the army since he was seventeen, he had been in the American war from the beginning at Lexington. At Bunker's Hill, as a lieutenant, he had distinguished himself by leading the grenadiers of his company after his captain had fallen. He had seen active duty in the principal battles of the north from Long Island to Monmouth and in the south from Charlestown to Camden.[41] Rawdon, however, bore a reputation for condoning the brutal conduct of the British army. He had written on September 25, 1776, while in New York, "I think we should (whenever we get further into the country) give free liberty to the soldiers to ravage it at will, that these infatuated creatures may feel what a calamity war is."[42]

There is little evidence that Rawdon had changed his attitude since the winter of 1776 and 1777 when he made his flippant remark:

> The fair nymphs of this isle [Staten Island] were in wonderful tribulation, as the fresh meat our men have got here has made them riotous as satyrs. A girl cannot step into the bushes to pluck a rose without runing the most imminent risk of being ravished, and they are so little accustomed to these vigorous methods they don't bear them with the proper resignation, and of consequence we have most entertaining court-martials every day.[43]

Rawdon, however, defended his part in Hayne's execution in his reply to Henry Lee. In his letter Rawdon was able to give himself an air of detached objectivity that the records do not substantiate. There can be no denying the cruelty on both sides of the war from "Tarleton's quarter" to the aftermath of King's Mountain. The depth of Rawdon's involvement in the Hayne affair is revealed nevertheless in the letter in which he compared Hayne's execution to that of Major John André. André was a British officer captured behind American lines out of uniform carrying documents relating to Benedict Arnold and the planned capitulation of West Point. André was executed as a spy. Rawdon's comparison of the two men gives credence to the story that the petitions of the ladies of Charlestown on behalf of Hayne were cancelled by Rawdon with the words "Major André."[44]

Colonel Balfour was popularly depicted as an arrogant upstart, son of a Scottish bookseller, and as having fought the Revolution inside the gates of Charlestown. In fact, Balfour distinguished himself at Bunker's Hill, where he was severely wounded, and at Long Island and Brooklyn. He was also present at the battles of Elizabethtown, Brandywine and Germantown; and, after the capture of Charlestown, Balfour was commandant at Ninety Six. After Patterson was forced by illness to return to New York, Balfour became commandant at Charlestown. There he obeyed to the letter the orders of Cornwallis.[45]

To understand Rawdon's and Balfour's decision, it is essential to examine British policy in South Carolina. In August of 1780 the Patriots had intercepted a message from Cornwallis to Colonel

Courtesy **The State** *Newspaper.*

Major John André was a British officer executed as a spy in the Benedict Arnold affair. André's execution was later mentioned by Lord Rawdon in an attempt to justify that of Hayne. This silhouette was cut by André.

Cruger, commandant of Ninety Six, an officer in the provincials. The letter described the action at Camden and described a firm manner of treating rebels:

> I have given orders that all the inhabitants of this province, who had submitted, and who have taken part in this revolt, should be punished with the greatest rigour, that they should be imprisoned, and their whole property taken from them or destroyed; I have likewise directed that compensation should be made out of their effects to the persons who have been plundered and oppressed by them. I have ordered in the most positive manner, that every militia man who had borne arms with us and had afterwards joined the enemy should be immediately hanged. I have now, Sir, only to desire that you will take the most vigorous measures to extinguish the rebellion in the district in which you command, and that you will obey in the strictest manner the directions I have given in this letter, relative to the treatment of the country.[46]

The Whigs into whose hands the letter had fallen decided to use the informal letter and to reword it to read more as a statement of policy:

> I have given Orders that all the Inhabitants of this Province who have subscribed, and have taken Part in this Revolt, should be punished with the greatest Rigour, and also those who will not turn out, that they may be imprisoned, and their whole Property taken from them or destroyed. I have likewise ordered that Compensation should be made out of their Effects, to the Persons who have been injured and oppressed by them. I have ordered in the most positive Manner that every Militia Man, who has born Arms with us and afterwards joined the Enemy shall be immediately hanged. I desire you will take the most rigorous Measures to punish the Rebels in the District in which you command, and that you will obey in the strictest Manner the Directions I have given in this Letter Relative to the Inhabitants of this Country.[47]

The altered letter was addressed to Balfour, instead of to Cruger, because Balfour was a regular officer and it would incense public opinion to make a regular officer seem merciless. Copies were distributed around the countryside and sent to George Washington, as was Rawdon's captured letter to Colonel Henry Rugely.[48] The impact of this order on the Patriots, at least on their attitude toward the British, is shown in Moultrie's description of the order as one that "let loose the dogs of war upon the poor inhabitants."[49] Lieutenant Colonel Thomas Brown, Tory commander at Augusta, had been tarred and feathered on August 2, 1775, by the Sons of Liberty and, using Cornwallis' order as an excuse for his revenge, hanged five men without a trial. A month later on September 18, 1780, he is said to have executed thirteen wounded prisoners.[50]

Cornwallis himself was aware that the order had been changed, but Governor Rutledge points out that, allowing for all the changes that were made, the effect of the letter was the same. The historian William Johnson said that he had evidence in his possession that Cornwallis "had inflicted death, for the offence of taking up arms, after giving a military parole to remain quietly at home." Cornwallis wrote on November 10, 1780, in a letter to General William Smallwood, commander of the First Maryland Brigade under Gates, "I am not conscious that any persons have been executed by us, unless *for bearing arms after giving a military parole to remain quietly at home*; or for enrolling themselves voluntarily in our militia, receiving arms and ammunition from the king's store, and taking the first opportunity for joining our enemies. The only persons hanged at Camden, after the actions of the 16th and 18th, except some deserters from our army, were *two or three* of the latter description who were picked out of about *thirty* convicted for the like offence, on account of some particularly aggravating circumstances which attended their cases."[51]

William Moultrie, who apparently was not aware that the letter had been intercepted, cited it as the general order under which Hayne was executed.[52] Balfour in a letter to General Greene referred to an order from Cornwallis. He asserted that the execution "took place by the joint order of Lord Rawdon and myself, in consequence of the most express directions from Lord Cornwallis to us, in regard to all those who shall be found in arms, after being at their own request, received as subjects, . . . more especially such as should have accepted of commissions, or might distinguish themselves in inducing a revolt of the country.[53] Isaac Hayne was, however, the most prominent man executed under this policy, and in the next chapter we shall examine the implications of his death.

Footnotes, Chapter II

[1]Christopher Ward, *The War of the Revolution,* (New York: MacMillan Co., 1952), II, 798-799; William B. Willcox, ed., *The American Rebellion: Sir Henry Clinton's Narrative of His Campaigns, 1775-1782,with an Appendix of Original Documents,* (New Haven: Yale University Press, 1954), pp. 508-509, 512-513; and Howard Peckham, *The War for Independence: A Military History,* (Chicago: University of Chicago Press, 1958), pp. 145-155.

[2]Ward, *The War of the Revolution,* II, 798-799. Rawdon wrote Cornwallis on May 24, 1781, after evacuating Camden, "On the 7th May Lieutenant Colonel Watson joined me with his detachment (at Camden), much reduced in number through casualties, sickness, and a reinforcement which he had left to strengthen the garrison at Georgetown. By him I received the unwelcome intelligence that the whole interior country had revolted, and that Marion and Lee, after reducing a post at Wright's Bluff, had crossed the Santee to support the insurgents...." Camden was evacuated and, when he arrived at Nelson's Ferry, Rawdon learned that Fort Motte, with his provisions, had fallen. Willcox, ed., *The American Rebellion,* pp. 521-522.

[3]Willcox, ed., *The American Rebellion,* pp. 521-522; Benjamin Franklin Stevens, ed., *The Campaign in Virginia, 1781: An Exact Reprint of Six Rare Pamphlets on the Clinton-Cornwallis Controversy,* (London: Charing Cross, 1888), I, 484.

[4]David Ramsay, *History of the Revolution of South Carolina,* (Trenton: Isaac Collins, 1785), II, 543-545.

[5]Rawdon wrote Cornwallis: "General Greene invested Ninety-six on the 22d of May. All my letters to Lieutenant Colonel Cruger failed, so that he thought himself bound to maintain that post. Fortunately we are now in a condition to undertake succoring him without exposing a more valuable stake. On the 3d instant the fleet from Ireland arrived, having on board the Third, Nineteenth, and Thirtieth Regiments, a detachment of the Guards, and a considerable body of recruits. I shall march on the 7th toward Ninety-Six, having been reinforced by the flank companies of the three regiments. If I am in time to save that post, it will be fortunate circumstance." Willcox, ed., *The American Rebellion,* p. 527.

[6] Ward, *The War of the Revolution,* II, 813.

[7] Ward, *The War of the Revolution,* II, 823-825.

[8] A letter from Rawdon to Cornwallis gives a detailed account of Rawdon's march to Ninety Six and his subsequent withdrawal: "I left Stewart to command on the Frontier; making the Congaree and Santee our boundaries during the continuance of the Heat. And the total failure of my health obliges me now with great respect to make use of the leave of absence which the Commander in Chief had the goodness to present me at the beginning of the year." Rawdon to Cornwallis, August 2, 1781, Cornwallis Papers, PRO 30/11/7, Microfilm, South Carolina Department of Archives and History. See also Willard M. Wallace, *Appeal to Arms: A Military History of the American Revolution,* (New York: Harper and Brothers, 1951), p. 242.

[9] Balfour to Cornwallis, April 26, 1781, Cornwallis Papers, PRO 30/11/6, Microfilm, South Carolina Department of Archives and History. Harden wrote Marion on April 7, 1781, "I have been able to keep from Purisburg to Pon Pon clear, that two or three men may ride in safety, and would have gone lower down, but was in hopes you would have been over the river and been in their rear, when we might have been sure of them." On April 18 Harden wrote Marion about the surrender of Fort Balfour at Pocotaligo, with "one Militia Colonel, one Major, three Captains, three Lieutenants, and sixty privates of Col. Fenwick's, one Lieutenant and 22 dragoons and their horses." Robert W. Gibbes, *Documentary History of the American Revolution,* (Columbia: Banner Steam-Power Press, 1853), III, 50, 55.

[10] Willcox, ed., *The American Rebellion,* p. 520.

[11] William Moultrie, *Memoirs of the American Revolution,* (New York: David Longworth, 1802), II, 291; Edward McCrady, *The History of South Carolina in the Revolution, 1780-1783,* (New York: MacMillan Co., 1902), pp. 544-545.

[12] *Royal Gazette,* (Charlestown), July 25-28, 1781.

[13] Willcox, ed., *The American Rebellion.* p. 549.

[14] Gibbes, *Documentary History of the American Revolution,* III, 51, 55.

[15] Henry Lee, *Memoirs of the War in the Southern Department of the United States,* (New York: University Publishing Co., 1869), p. 452.

[16] John Rutledge in describing the reasons Hayne took up arms said, " . . . Our People, after having got possession of the Country below where Col. Hayne resided, insisted that he shd. resume the Command which he formerly held of the Colleton County Regiment of Militia, &, if he had not done so, he wd., probably, have been brought off, & treated, as a Prisoner, perhaps harshly." John Rutledge to John Dickinson, Letters Relating to Isaac Hayne, Manuscript Collection, Library Company of Philadelphia.

[17] Accounts Audited, Nos. 538, 4597, 6748, 7931 and 8748, South Carolina Department of Archives and History.

[18] McCrady, *The History of South Carolina in the Revolution, 1780-1783,* p. 319. Rawdon said, "The insulting triumph with which Mr. Williamson was told,

that the purpose in capturing him, was to have been hanged in the camp of General Greene, had naturally roused the indignation of all the friends of the British Government." Lee, *Memoirs of the War,* p. 618.

[19] Balfour to Clinton, July 21, 1781, Cornwallis Papers, PRO 30/11/109, Microfilm, South Carolina Department of Archives and History. Rutledge wrote that Hayne treated Williamson like a gentleman and "immediately gave him his parole to Charles-town." John Rutledge to John Dickinson, Letters Relating to Isaac Hayne, Manuscript Collection, Library Company of Philadelphia.

[20] Christopher Ward, *The War of the Revolution,* II, 798-799; Moultrie, *Memoirs of the American Revolution,* II, 300; and Lee, *Memoirs of the War,* II, 616.

[21] McCrady, *The History of South Carolina in the Revolution, 1780-1783,* 387-388; Ramsay, *History of the Revolution of South Carolina,* II, 511- 512. Ramsay said there were four general officers and five captains.

[22] Lee, *Memoirs of the War,* p. 617.

[23] McCrady, *The History of South Carolina in the Revolution, 1780-1783,* p. 388.

[24] *The New-Hampshire Gazette and General Advertiser,* Vol. XXVI, no. 1303, October 20, 1781; Ramsay, *History of the Revolution of South Carolina,* II, 513-515. The wording of the documents varies somewhat in these two sources, *e.g.,* "tribunal" instead of "council of war".

[25] McCrady, *The History of South Carolina in the Revolution, 1780-1783,* p. 388.

[26] McCrady, *The History of South Carolina in the Revolution, 1780-1783,* pp. 392-393; Ramsay, *The History of the Revolution of South Carolina,* II, 515, 518-521.

[27] Rawdon said of Balfour, "He solicited my concurrence (absolutely ineffective in any other point of view, in a district where I was wholly under his control)...." Lee, *Memoirs of the War,* p. 616.

[28] Rawdon explained that his reference to Greene had been misunderstood and that he had merely meant that, if Greene interceded, Rawdon would not be able to get Hayne off. Lee, *Memoirs of the War,* p. 617.

[29] Ramsey, *The History of the Revolution of South Carolina,* II, 516-517.

[30] John Rutledge to John Dickinson, Letters Relating to Isaac Hayne, Manuscript Collection, Library Company of Philadelphia; Ramsay, *The History of the Revolution of South Carolina,* II, 282, 508-511. John Scott, a "distressed exile from his native Country" and a former merchant in Charlestown, asked leniency for "his activity in promoting a petition in favor of the unfortunate Coll. Haines exerting all his Interest and using every means in his power in endeavors to save him." A letter was included from Isaac Harleston to Colonel Pinckney dated February 5, 1783, which said "Mr. John McQueen, Capt. James Ladson and Messrs. Pringle, are witnesses of his exertions to avert the fate of the unfortunate Col. Hayne." Confiscated Estates Manuscripts, Petitions of John Scott, South Carolina Department of Archives and History. Rawdon said, "A

petition to be signed by the ladies, was drawn up as a step gratifying to me, by one of the officers of the staff (I believe by Major Barry, the deputy adjutant-general) to serve as a basis for my address to the commandant." Lee, *Memoirs of the War,* p. 616.

[31] Lorenzo Sabine, *Biographical Sketches of Loyalists of the American Revolution with an Historical Essay,* (Boston: Little, Brown and Co., 1864), II, 459. Rawdon explained the petitions thus: "Mr. Alexander Wright and Mr. Powell . . . ., in compliance with my wishes, undertook to try whether a petition for pardon to Hayne might not be procured from a respectable number of loyalists; though they gave me little encouragement to hope success, from even their known and just influence with that body. They first applied to Lieutenant-Governor Bull, who consented to sign the petition, provided the Attorney-General, Sir Egerton Leigh, would do so. The answer of Leigh was, *that he would burn his hand off rather than do an act so injurious to the king's service.* Lieutenant-Governor Bull's conditional promise of course fell to the ground, though he subsequently, from some dupery practised upon his age, joined his name with those of certain of your most active and avowed partisans; and not one loyalist of repute could be persuaded to put his name on the petition." Lee, *Memoirs of the War,* p. 617. Isaac Neufville delivered a disposition stating in part "That the Deponent was informed that at the intercession of several persons among whom were many British officers he was respited for 48 hours. That a Petition for his pardon was signed and presented by those gentlemen to the Commandant but without effect." Worthington C. Ford and Gaillard Hunt, eds., *Journals of the Continental Congress, 1774-1789,* (Washington: Government Printing Office, 1912), XXI, 927.

[32] Sabine, *Biographical Sketches of Loyalists in the American Revolution,* II, 9; McCowen, *The British Occupation of Charleston,* p. 18.

[33] William Edward Hayne wrote in 1835, "I recollect also going with my brother Isaac & sister Sarah in Company with my Aunt Peronneau to Lieut. Col. Balfour...and... on our knees presenting a petition to him in favor of my father but without effect." William Edward Hayne to Jeremiah A. Yates, Charleston, December 23, 1835, William Edward Hayne Manuscript, South Caroliniana Library.

[34] William Edward Hayne to Jeremiah A. Yates, Charleston, December 23, 1835, William Edward Hayne Manuscript, South Caroliniana Library.

[35] Worthington C. Ford and Gaillard Hunt, eds., *Journals of the Continental Congress, 1774-1789,* (Washington: Government Printing Office, 1912), XXI, 927.

[36] A.S. Salley, Jr., "Capt. John Colcock and Some of his Descendants," *South Carolina Historical and Genealogical Magazine,* III (1902), 220.

[37] Ramsay, *History of the Revolution,* II, 283-284. In a footnote to a poem written by William Gilmore Simms in 1858, Hayne's execution is described: "The military escort consisted of three hundred men. The place of execution was just without the city-lines, near *Radcliffe's Garden,* nearly in front, and within

a stone's throw of the present Orphan House Building. The troops formed a hollow square around the scaffold, the British troops occupying the front and rear, the Hessians on the right and left." "Hayne: A Dirge," *Russell's Magazine,* IV (December, 1858), 247-248. See Appendix I.

[38] According to Rawdon, Balfour had written to him that "an insurrection had taken place in the rear of my army, but had luckily been crushed. He stated that the imperious necessity of repressing the disposition to similar acts of treachery, by making an example of the individual who had planned, as well as headed the revolt, and who had fallen into Lieutenant-Colonel Balfour's hands." Lee, *Memoirs of the War,* p. 616, Balfour to Clinton, July 21, 1781, Cornwallis Papers, PRO 30/11/109.

[39] *Royal Gazette* (Charlestown), May 17, 1781. William Charles Wells, born in Charlestown, was the son of Robert Wells, who was the printer of the *Royal Gazette* and the largest bookseller in pre-Revolutionary South Carolina. Wells was a physician and in 1781 was supporting the British cause as "an officer in a corps of volunteers, a printer, a bookseller, a merchant, and a trustee of parties in England." Lorenzo Sabine, *Biographical Sketches of Loyalists of the American Revolution,* (Boston: Little, Brown and Co., 1864), II, 408. In an autobiographical reminiscence Wells said that he wrote a work on parole violations at Balfour's request, which made Balfour and Rawdon feel justified "in putting to death a Colonel Haynes." William Charles Wells, *Two Essays: One upon Single Vision with Two Eyes: the other on Dew,* (London: Printed for Archibald Constable and Co., Edinburgh, 1818), p. xliv. Dr. Calhoun Winton of the University of Maryland English Department discovered and kindly furnished this reference.

[40] In describing the British officers in the American Revolution, J.W. Fortesque said, "The ablest of all was Lord Rawdon, who received his baptism of fire at twenty-one, on Bunker's Hill, and at twenty-six contrived with great skill to save the position abandoned by Cornwallis." J.W. Fortesque, *A History of the British Army,* (London: MacMillan and Co., 1902), III, 414.

[41] Leslie Stephen and Sidney Lee, eds., *The Dictionary of National Biography,* (London: Oxford University Press, 1949-1950), IX, 117-122.

[42] John Shy, "The American Revolution: The Military Conflict Considered as a Revolutionary War," *Essays on the American Revolution,* Stephen G. Kurtz and James H. Hutson, eds., (New York: W.W. Norton and Co., Inc., 1973), p. 135.

[43] Peckham, *The War for Independence,* p. 47.

[44] William Oliver Stevens, *Charleston: Historic City of Gardens,* (New York: Dodd, Mead and Co., 1939), p. 142. See also Margaret Hayne Harrison, *A Charleston Album.* (Rindge, New Hampshire: Richard R. Smith, Inc., 1953), p. 49.

[45] Stephens and Lee, eds., *Dictionary of National Biography,* I, 976-977.

[46] Franklin and Mary B. Wickwire, *Cornwallis: The American Adventure,* (Boston: Houghton Mifflin Co., 1970), p. 179.

[47] Wickwire, *Cornwallis: The American Adventure,* p. 180.

[48] According to Ramsay and McCrady this proclamation was addressed to the commander of Ninety Six, with similar ones sent to the other posts. Ramsay cites the specific examples of a number of men, five of whom were named, who were hanged at Camden. Ramsay, *History of the Revolution of South-Carolina,* II, 156-159; McCrady, *History of South Carolina in the Revolution, 1775-1780,* pp. 709-711. The Wickwires, who favor Cornwallis, take a more tolerant view of him and say that he had earlier pardoned three men who had broken their oaths. Wickwire, *Cornwallis: The American Adventure,* pp. 176-182.

[49] Moultrie, *Memoirs of the American Revolution,* II, 241.

[50] McCrady, *History of South Carolina in the Revolution, 1775-1780,* pp. 723-733, 737-738; Kenneth Coleman, *The American Revolution in Georgia, 1763-1789,* (Athens: University of Georgia Press, 1958), pp. 65, 134.

[51] William Johnson, *Sketches of the Life and Correspondence of Nathanael Greene,* (Charleston: A. E. Miller, 1822), II, 467.

[52] Moultrie, *Memoirs of the American Revolution,* II, 241.

[53] Gibbes, *Documentary History of the American Revolution,* III, 133-134. Balfour wrote Greene on September 3, 1781.

Chapter Three
Implications and Aftereffects

On August 8 the people of Charlestown read the result of Rawdon's and Balfour's decision in the *Royal Gazette*: Isaac Hayne had been executed as a traitor.[1] Had Hayne been granted a trial, however, he could have offered any of several defenses.[2] In light of the circumstances of his execution and the British conditions in South Carolina at the time, the question arises of why Hayne had to die. The greater his prestige and that of those pleading for his life, the greater the impact of his death would be. The British situation had been deteriorating, and Hayne's death intimidated many of those who had joined the Americans.

Governor Rutledge's letter to the South Carolina delegates in Congress demonstrated the temporary success of the execution as a tactic to discourage the partisan bands: "The Excn' of Hayne had the Effect wch the Enemy foresaw, & expected, that unparalled piece of Cruelty- & indeed, a much greater Effect than you can conceive, for, a great many Protection Men, who had joined Harden, thereupon deserted him & again submitted themselves, to the British Government & Mercy, so that, when Marion went last, to the Southward, Harden had not 50 Men, in Arms, & had it not been, for Marions Appearance in that Quarter, & his Support & Countenance, at such a critical Period, Hardens Force wd. have been reduced much lower —."[3] The result of the hanging had the temporary effect of halting the militia from joining the Americans, but the later cries for retaliation whetted the appetite for war.

Painting by Peale, Courtesy South Caroliniana Library

Nathanael Greene (1742-1786) was the commander of American forces in the South. His threat to retaliate for Hayne's execution insured that no other executions would be carried out in the South for the duration of the war.

General Nathanael Greene, commander of the American forces in the South and the man on whom the responsibility for retaliation for Hayne's death fell, received word of the execution six days later on August 10.[4] Although Greene knew that public outrage demanded retribution, other considerations hobbled him. First, he believed that the retaliation should be against a British rather than a Tory officer. He feared that the British would like to see the Whigs and Tories eliminate each other. The second and more immediate consideration was for the sixty-two citizens of Charlestown who had been held at St. Augustine and who were being exchanged. Greene awaited their safe return to make his intention to retaliate known to the British.

The day Greene, camped on the High Hills of Santee, received news of Hayne's death, he wrote Francis Marion. Marion had himself already threatened reprisals because of the injuries his men had suffered from the British. Greene assured him that he would inquire into Hayne's death and, if he received no satisfaction, would give no quarter to British officers whom he captured.[5]

As Greene waited for the safe return of the prisoners, Hayne was not forgotten. Governor John Rutledge wrote Marion from the High Hills of Santee on August 13 requesting him to send to Colonel Harden for a "full and authentic account of the execution of Col. Hayne, with every material circumstance relative to that unhappy affair."[6] The governor wanted Congress to have copies of the papers pertaining to Hayne. These documents were letters exchanged between Hayne and Balfour, the petition of the women of Charlestown on Hayne's behalf to Balfour, and the speech of Hayne to his regiment urging them not to plunder.

To some, however, the American reaction was unnecessarily slow. A week later, on August 20, the officers under Greene signed a statement condemning the "commanding officer of the British forces in Charleston" for his treatment of prisoners in holding them aboard prison ships, for his discriminating in the exchange of militia officers, and finally for his condoning the execution of Hayne. They requested a strict inquiry and, if warranted, they urged retaliation in a similar manner on British subjects. The petition was signed by all the officers with the exception of Colonel

Henry Lee, who was detached to the banks of the Congaree at the time.[7]

After Greene received word that the prisoners from St. Augustine had arrived safely, he announced his intention to retaliate. He realized, however, that the execution of Hayne raised "some important questions of allegiance and the rights of punishment and the obligation of subjects."[8] On August 25 Greene wrote to the President of Congress for approval of the measures he was taking. He stopped all further exchanges of prisoners, avowed his intention of retaliating and issued a proclamation explaining these measures. He expressed no doubt that Congress would approve the steps he had taken no matter what their consequences might be.[9]

The next day Greene issued the proclamation to which he had referred in his letters. In it he stated his "intention to make reprisals for all such inhuman insults as often as they take place." He lamented the "necessity I am under of having recourse to measures so extremely wounding to the sentiments of humanity, and so contrary to the liberal principles upon which I wish to conduct the war."[10] In letters written the same day to Cornwallis, Balfour and George Washington, Greene elaborated on his proclamation and again expressed his resolve that the British would not go unpunished for the act. In his letter to Cornwallis, Greene interrupted the exchange of prisoners agreed to by them in the cartel of May, 1781,[11] He furthermore warned Cornwallis that Americans would "retaliate for every violence offered to their adherents." He wanted the British general to indicate that he disapproved of the execution of Hayne.[12]

In his letter to Balfour, Greene referred to other breaches in the cartel. He promised immediate retaliation for Hayne's death if it were not better justified than it had been so far. Not only would he retaliate for Hayne but also for any other American who was treated in that manner in the future.[13] In a letter to Washington, Greene reiterated his determination to retaliate, calling the execution a "flagrant violation" of the cartel.[14]

Greene hoped also that the proclamation he issued would sufficiently reassure the militiamen that they might not abandon the army as a group.[15] Governor Rutledge's letter to the Continental

Congress demonstrated how Harden's men had left. Greene correctly anticipated that the proclamation would partly nullify the effects of Hayne's execution. When the militia returned, it was often with a greater hatred of the British as "pity and revenge sharpened the swords of the countrymen and friends of the much beloved sufferer."[16]

Marion, who had gone into the area where Hayne had lived to help Harden, on August 30 ambushed Major Thomas Fraser and his Loyalists on Fraser's return from an excursion over the Pon Pon to harass the Whigs who lived there. The resulting losses for Major Fraser, who had captured Hayne, were Marion's private revenge.[17] In addition to the one hundred killed and wounded of the enemy, Marion had helped dispel the fear that had depleted the ranks of the militia after Hayne's execution.

Governor Rutledge wrote about the success of the ambush: "Happily Marion's putting Fraser to flight, has given the Southward-Militia. (Most of whom had taken Protection, especially those in the lower part of the Country,) fresh, Spirits- & Gen. Greene's well timed Proclamation, & spirited Determination, in Consequence of Hayne's Death, has removed the Apprehension of our Militia, of suffering in like Manner, if taken Prisoner — This measure, & the steps taken with our Militia, will, I hope, soon get a respectable Number into the Field."[18]

Greene resolved not to be hasty in retaliating since no one else had been executed. He wanted to know the opinions of Congress on the measures he had taken. On Wednesday August 29, John Mathews, South Carolina delegate to the Continental Congress, made a motion in Congress that due to the execution of Hayne by "the officer, commanding the troops of his Britannic Majesty, in the State of South Carolina" that "a British officer, now a prisoner within these United States in the line of the British army not under the rank of Major immediately to suffer the same death that was inflicted on Col. Haynes." The motion was referred to a committee of three.

The committee reported on August 31 the resolve that Greene inquire into the circumstances of Hayne's death and that "if thereupon it shall appear that such execution was contrary to the laws of war, he cause retaliation to be made in such manner, as is

51

warranted by those laws, and will in his opinion have the most probable tendency to restrain the enemy from such acts of cruelty in future." It was ordered on September 7 that the report of the committee on the information respecting Hayne be referred back to the committee. Again on September 10 the committee delivered a report respecting Hayne. Congress resolved on September 18 "that the conduct of Major General Greene, in taking necessary measures for retaliation, be, and, hereby is approved."[19] Nathanael Greene, as we shall see later, interpreted this to mean only that Congress had approved the action that he had taken thus far.

Greene received a reply from Balfour in early September. Balfour justified the execution of Hayne as taking place "by joint order of Lord Rawdon and myself, in consequence of the most express directions from Lord Cornwallis to us, in regard to all those who shall be found in arms, after being at their own request received as British subjects."[20]

Greene in his reply to Balfour on September 14 enclosed a copy of a letter to Cornwallis of the previous December 17 condemning the order to which Balfour referred. In his letter to Balfour, Greene went further into his feelings about retaliation. "Retaliation presupposes an act of violence having been committed, and that it is adopted to punish the past and restrain the future, and, therefore, whatever will produce these consequences is warranted by the laws of retaliation."[21] Ironically events had taken place, and were about to take place, in consequence of which retaliation would be neither necessary nor advisable to serve these ends. Greene was, in essence, explaining why he ultimately would not redress the wrong.

Greene did not want the retaliation for Hayne to lead to a disregard of the laws of war by both sides with death avenged by death. He had sought from Cornwallis some disapproval of the action of the British officers who had executed Hayne. Cornwallis replied on September 15 that he could not be expected to condemn Balfour before he heard his side. Cornwallis cautioned Greene: "I trust that you will take time to investigate this business with coolness and temper before you proceed to retaliation as the consequences of it may be very fatal to many innocent individuals on both sides." [22] The exchange of prisoners was suspended, with each side holding hostages against the threat of retaliation by the other.

The Battle of Eutaw Springs on September 8 delivered to the Americans enough British officers virtually to assure that no one else would be hanged by the British. Unfortunately the battle also brought the capture of Lieutenant Colonel William Washington, the cavalry commander who had signed the August 20 petition to Greene urging retaliation which, if carried out, would now endanger his own life.[23] On October 19 Cornwallis surrendered at Yorktown, giving the Americans a vast number of prisoners, though they were protected by the terms of their surrender.[24]

A few days after Washington's capture, Governor Thomas Burke of North Carolina and every Continental and militia officer with him at Hillsborough were seized by a band of Loyalists. Burke was taken to Wilmington and then sent to Charlestown. He became, in effect, a hostage against retaliation for Hayne's death. The British needed a prisoner of Burke's importance because Lord Rawdon had been captured by the French after he left Charlestown for England on August 21.[25] Christopher Gadsden, lieutenant governor of South Carolina, and four members of the Privy Council wrote the Continental Congress suggesting that Rawdon, then a prisoner, should be the subject of retaliation.[26]

Any doubt that prisoners were being held for that eventuality was soon dispelled. The letters between the commandant at Wilmington, Major James Craig, and Alexander Martin, a North Carolina senator who requested Burke's parole, were sent to American newspapers. To Martin's request Craig replied that Burke was a "state and not a military prisoner." Because of this Burke was subject to trial for treason. Craig continued in his letter that he normally would have paroled the Continental officers he held but "for a threat which has been held out in South-Carolina of retaliating on the persons of the British officers [for] the execution of a Mr. Hayne."[27]

On October 25 Greene wrote George Washington about the condition of the Southern army after the Battle of Eutaw Springs. Still on his mind, however, was the Hayne affair. He sent a copy of all the "letters and papers that have passed respecting Col.

Hayne's execution" by courier. Although Washington had been informed earlier of the circumstances, Greene now wanted him to be particularly aware of all its ramifications "as the business, in its consequences, might involve the whole Continent and particularly the military part; and, therefore, would ultimately rest" with Washington.[28]

The next month Greene again urged Washington that "something decisive" had to be done respecting Hayne. Because of the international implications of retaliation, he wanted to proceed on the orders of the commander-in-chief and Congress. Congress had approved only the measures Greene had taken so far. He did not feel that he could have retaliated without the consent of Congress unless there was an immediate threat that the offense might be repeated. Greene also related that he did not have an officer of equal rank with Hayne in his possession but would retaliate on anyone that Congress thought appropriate.[29]

On December 9, as he had the month before, Greene expressed essentially the same feelings to Congress about the authority given him to act. He requested a clarification of their intention. However, the letter was not read in Congress until January 29, 1782, when it was referred to the "committee appointed to confer with the Commander-in-Chief."[30] In a February 19 letter to Colonel John Laurens, who was to meet with a British commissioner, Greene urged him to mention that the matter of retaliation was before Congress at that time. His message continued with the warning that "a repetition of the like violence to any militia adhering to our cause will produce an immediate retaliation, not only for the second but the first offence."[31]

Members of the South Carolina delegation to the Continental Congress saw in Cornwallis' capture a chance to retaliate for the death of Hayne. On October 25 Arthur Middleton made a motion, seconded by Isaac Motte, that "General Washington be directed to detain Earl Cornwallis, and the officers captured in the garrisons of York and Gloucester till the further order of Congress." Elias Boudinot, a delegate to the Continental Congress from New Jersey, wrote of the heated debate that followed the motion. He said that the delegates from South Carolina charged Cornwallis

Charles Lord Cornwallis (1738-1805) was commander of British forces in the South, and left South Carolina early in 1781. Cornwallis' order to execute those found in arms after being received as British subjects was used by Nisbet Balfour to justify the death of Hayne.

with many cruelties in the state, particularly the murder of Isaac Hayne. The motion was made that Washington execute Cornwallis in retaliation for Hayne, and it was strongly supported. It was defeated only after the delegates understood that such a measure would place Washington in an embarrassing position because of the terms of Cornwallis' surrender. When the final vote was taken, South Carolina was the only state to affirm the motion.[32]

In the middle of December Washington gave Greene a reply to his request concerning retaliation: "I really know not what to say on the subject of Retaliation. Congress have it under consideration and we must await their determination. Of this I am convinced, that of all Laws it is the most difficult to execute, where you have not the transgressor himself in your possession. Humanity will ever interfere and plead strongly against the sacrifice of an innocent person for the guilt of another."[33] This word of caution offered further encouragement for Greene to take no action. Washington himself was to find the truth of his statement during the next year when he would face the prospect of retaliating for the execution of Captain Joshua Huddy by Loyalists.[34]

Greene had turned to two sources for guidance in the Hayne affair—to Congress and to the commander-in-chief. The response of each lessened the chances of retaliation for Isaac Hayne's death. Congress, by delaying a response to Greene's inquiries, showed itself to be in no mood to increase hostilities as peace seemed to be approaching. Greene, following Washington's suggestion that only the perpetrator of a crime should be punished for it, knew that the imprisonment of Governor Burke by the British ensured that Rawdon and Balfour would not be punished. Governor Burke had no doubt that his life was in danger and that the British might soon be "acting on me a Tragedy Similar to that on Col. Haynes."[35] When he was paroled to James Island, he was so fearful that retaliation on him would be forthcoming, or that the Tories would shoot him in the back, that he broke parole and returned to North Carolina.[36]

Lord Rawdon was held on the Chesapeake after his capture by the French. Following Yorktown he was taken to Brest, France, where he was paroled. In a letter to his uncle, Lord Huntington, Rawdon related his good treatment by the French Admiral de

Grasse. He attributed their attitude to his having told them the proceedings of Hayne's court-martial, of which, he wrote, de Grasse and his officers approved completely.[37]

Although Rawdon was not exchanged until June of 1782, he had been permitted to return to England early in 1782.[38] On August 15, 1781, before he left Charlestown, Rawdon had received an enthusiastic farewell from many of the Loyalist citizens of the city.[39] The reception that he was to receive upon his return to England was somewhat different. Soon after he arrived, Rawdon learned that the Duke of Richmond intended to denounce Hayne's execution in the House of Lords on January 31, 1782. John Bowman of Charlestown had sent the Duke of Richmond, who favored the American cause and criticized official British policy, an account of the execution.[40] The Duke of Richmond in turn sent the papers to Henry Laurens, who was recuperating at Bath after his ordeal in the Tower of London. Laurens confirmed that the papers agreed with the account he had heard. The inhabitants of Charlestown had "commisserated" with Hayne and could not blame him for taking arms. Even "living peaceably under the parole or protection which had been granted him," he was subjected to British depredations in the countryside; and his own home had been frequently plundered.[41] However, after considerable debate and public controversy, the move to censure Rawdon was defeated seventy-three to twenty-five. The Earl of Huntington led the men who defended his nephew. An exchange of letters between Rawdon and the Duke of Richmond followed. Rawdon demanded and received an apology from the Duke upon the threat of defending his honor with the sword.[42]

While Lord Rawdon faced censure in England, Balfour found his situation increasingly difficult in Charlestown. General Leslie, in a letter to General Clinton on March 30, reminded him of Balfour's discomfort in Charlestown since "the circumstances of Haine's execution renders his situation here very unpleasant."[43] Balfour remained in Charlestown until July of 1782, when he was transferred to New York. Balfour received the same expressions of appreciation when he left Charlestown that Rawdon had received on his departure.[44]

The subject of retaliation was renewed in February of 1782. Greene wrote General Leslie to learn his opinion of the execution of Hayne. While awaiting the decision of Congress, Greene wanted to continue the exchange of prisoners. Aware of Washington's opinion that Balfour and Rawdon alone were suitable subjects for retaliation, Greene prepared Clinton for what would surely be a decision not to retaliate by saying that if retaliation did not come, it would be "from the author's not being in our power."[45] General Leslie answered suggesting a meeting of representatives to discuss all differences. This meeting was "superceded by a general exchange negotiated in New York, and by the approach of peace."[46] As has been said of the settling of the question of retaliation, it was "closed rather by the close of the war itself, than by any special consideration of the subject."[47] Nevertheless, the subject was never laid to rest.

Greene, waiting to see if another execution seemed to be forthcoming, found that Hayne's death had been ineffectual in preventing the paroled Patriots from returning to the American cause. In fact many apparently fought with even greater zeal. Greene's threat to retaliate, as time bore out, proved to be a deterrent since no other executions were carried out in the South.

Although the execution of Huddy in New Jersey was not analogous to that of Hayne, Benjamin Franklin observed during the Asgill controversy that, "General Greene, though he solemnly and publicly promised it in a proclamation, never made any retaliation for the murder of Colonel Haynes and many others in Carolina, and the people, who now think if he had fulfilled his promise this crime would not have been committed, clamor so loudly that I doubt General Washington can not well refuse what appears to them so just and necessary for their common security."[48] Thomas Paine advised Washington that, because the execution of Huddy followed Hayne's so closely, much embarrassment would arise in England. He felt that Washington should hold Asgill's fate in suspension, thus appealing to a "greater quantity of their passions and vices,—and restrain them more than his execution." He astutely added that if the effect of an execution could be achieved without the execution it would look "infinitely better hereafter, when the sensations that now provoke, and the circumstances that would immediately justify his exit, shall be forgotten or but faintly remembered."[49] Ultimately Greene, after having written to both Congress and Washington, did not retaliate because the "threat of retaliation had produced all the beneficial effects that could have resulted from the execution of the threat."[50]

Was Hayne executed for reasons that were, if not justifiable, then at least understandable? Other men, Andrew Pickens, for example, had taken oaths of allegiance to Britain and then fought for the Patriot cause. In Hayne's case the records reveal that he had personal reasons for needing to remain out of the war. His wife, two children and at least four slaves were ill and later died of smallpox.[51] When the question of loyalty arose, Hayne chose that to his family before that to country or to king. The indications are that Hayne endured hardships while under his oath. His plantation was plundered and he was at the mercy of the British controlling that area.[52]

Pressure for Hayne to take an active part in the war came from the Americans as well as from the British. Colonel William Harden, militia leader in that area, knew that if Hayne forsook his oath, many of his neighbors would follow his example.[53] William Gilmore Simms' Colonel Richard Walton, a character in his novel *The Partisan,* was based on Hayne and illustrated an important aspect of Hayne's decision to break his oath: he was no longer able to remain neutral; he had to choose sides or face the threat of arrest or confiscation of his property by either party.[54]

The men who decided Hayne's fate, Rawdon and Balfour, were men in the public eye who felt personally justified in their action. As has been shown, the British situation in South Carolina at that time was precarious. Rawdon and Balfour executed Hayne under the pressure of the moment. This was evidenced later as, in the face of public censure, they felt the necessity to justify their action. The results following Hayne's execution showed it to be a senseless deed since his death only temporarily discouraged defections from British allegiance. In effect Isaac Hayne was sacrificed to the hopes of revitalizing the waning British effort in South Carolina. Although Rawdon and Balfour were both to have distinguished careers after the war, the death of Isaac Hayne remained a shadow in the past of each.

Footnotes, Chapter III

[1] *Royal Gazette* (Charlestown), August 8, 1781.

[2] William Dobein James, *A Sketch of the Life of Brigadier General Francis Marion,* (Marietta, Georgia: Continental Book Co., 1948). pp. 130-131.

[3] John Rutledge to the S.C. delegates in Congress, September 18, 1781, John Rutledge Letters, Charleston Library Society, Charleston, S.C. Hugh Rankin describes the reaction to Hayne's execution: "The execution of Hayne, however, did have a sobering effect and led to the reluctance of some militia to respond to calls. The Tories grew bolder. Some rode in large groups, as great as four or five hundred, rampaging through the countryside below Charleston. To furnish protection, Balfour sent Major Thomas Fraser and two hundred dragoons into the area." Hugh F. Rankin, *Francis Marion: The Swamp Fox,* (New York: Thomas Y. Crowell Co., 1973), p. 235. Edward McCrady, *The History of South Carolina in the Revolution, 1780-1783,* (New York: MacMillan Co., 1902), p. 434.

[4] Greene to Marion, August 10, 1781, in Robert W. Gibbes, ed., *Documentary History of the American Revolution,* (Columbia: Banner Steam-Power Press, 1853), III, 125.

[5] James, *A Sketch of the Life of Brigadier General Francis Marion,* p. 129; William Johnson, *Sketches of the Life and Correspondence of Nathanael Greene,* (Charleston: A.E. Miller, 1822), II, 189-190; Gibbes, *Documentary History of the American Revolution,* III, 126.

[6] Rutledge to Marion, August 13, 1781, in Gibbes, *Documentary History of the American Revolution,* III, 127.

[7] Officers of the Army to Greene, August 20, 1781, in Gibbes, *Documentary History of the American Revolution,* III, 128-129; David Ramsay, *The History of the Revolution of South Carolina From a British Province to an Independent State,* (Trenton: Isaac Collins, 1785), II, 285, 521-526; Johnson, *Sketches of the Life and Correspondence of Nathanael Greene,* II, 192-193; *Pennsylvania Packet,* September 16, 1781.

[8] Greene to the President of Congress, September 2, 1781, Papers of the Continental Congress, 1774-1789, no. 155, II, 267-268, National Archives Micro-

film, South Carolina Department of Archives and History; John Mathews to Greene, August 14, 1781, in Edmund C. Burnett, ed., *Letters of Members of the Continental Congress,* (Washington: Carnegie Institution, 1933), VI, 181-182.

[9] Greene to the President of Congress, August 25, 1781, Papers of the Continental Congress, no. 155, II, 241-242.

[10] Greene's Proclamation, August 26, 1781, in Gibbes, *Documentary History of the American Revolution,* III, 115-116; *Whitehall Evening-Post* (London), November 24, 1781.

[11] Greene explained in a letter to Lafayette, also written on August 26, that if he had not stopped the exchange of prisoners and issued the proclamation, the militia would have deserted in a body. Theodore G. Thayer, *Nathanael Greene: Strategist of the American Revolution,* (New York: Twayne, 1960), p. 372.

[12] Greene to Lord Cornwallis, August 26, 1781, Papers of the Continental Congress, no. 155, II, 287-288.

[13] Greene to Balfour, August 26, 1781, Papers of the Continental Congress, no. 155, II, 279-280.

[14] Jared Sparks, *Correspondence of the American Revolution,* (Boston: Little, Brown and Co., 1853), III, 393.

[15] Thayer, *Nathanael Greene: Strategist of the American Revolution,* p. 372.

[16] Ramsay, *The History of the Revolution of South Carolina,* II, 285.

[17] Robert D. Bass, *Gamecock: The Life and Campaigns of General Thomas Sumter,* (New York: Holt, Rinehart and Winston, 1961), p. 207; Rankin, *Francis Marion: The Swamp Fox,* pp. 237-238; and McCrady, *The History of South Carolina in the American Revolution, 1780-1783,* pp. 438-440.

[18] John Rutledge to the S.C. delegates in Congress, September 18, 1781, John Rutledge Letters, Charleston Library Society, Charleston, S.C.

[19] Worthington C. Ford and Gaillard Hunt, eds., *Journals of the Continental Congress, 1774-1789,* (Washington: Government Printing Office, 1912), XXI, 917-918, 927, 941, 972-973; Greene to the President of Congress, September 2, 1781, Papers of the Continental Congress, no. 155, II, 267-268.

[20] Balfour to Greene, September 3, 1781, Papers of the Continental Congress, no. 155, II, 341-344; Johnson, *Sketches of the Life and Correspondence of Nathanael Greene,* II, 193-194.

[21] Greene to Balfour, September 19, 1781, Papers of the Continental Congress, no. 155, II, 369-371.

[22] Cornwallis to Greene, September 15, 1781, Nathanael Greene Papers, General Correspondence, II, 167, Library of Congress Microfilm in South Carolina Department of Archives and History.

[23] William Washington, cousin of George Washington, was born in Stafford County, Virginia, in 1752. A cavalry officer, he was voted a silver medal by Congress for valor. After his capture he was held prisoner in Charlestown. He later married a local girl and settled there, where he was elected to the state

legislature. Saying he had no talent for making speeches, he declined to run for governor. Washington died in Charleston on March 6, 1810. McCrady, *South Carolina in the Revolution, 1780-1783,* pp. 454, 461. A Hessian officer, Carl Leopold Baurmeister, wrote from New York in October of 1781, after Greene's proclamation, "Should the right of retaliation be resorted to in such an unheard-of manner, many a colonel or other officer may be cruelly elevated sooner than could ever have been expected. Hence, Colonel Washington and others, it is reasonable to suppose, will be held as principal hostages." Bernhard A. Uhlendorf, trans., *Revolution in America: Confidential Letters and Journals 1776-1784 of Adjutant General Major Baurmeister of the Hessian Forces,* (New Brunswick: Rutgers University Press, 1957), pp. 468-469.

[24] Wickwire, *Cornwallis: The American Adventure,* p. 386; Johnson, *Sketches of the Life and Correspondence of Nathanael Greene,* II, 196.

[25] Balfour to Clinton, October 2, 1781, Cornwallis Papers, PRO 30/11/109, pp. 47-48; McCrady, *The History of South Carolina in the Revolution, 1780-1783,* pp. 465-466.

[26] The members of the Privy Council who signed the letter were Thomas Ferguson, Richard Hutson, David Ramsay and B. Cattell. Gadsden to S.C. delegates in the Continental Congress, September 17, 1781, in Richard Walsh, ed., *The Writings of Christopher Gadsden, 1746-1805,* (Columbia: University of South Carolina Press, 1966), p. 177.

[27] David Schenck, *North Carolina, 1780-81,* (Raleigh: Edwards and Broughton, 1889), p. 445; Martin to Craig, September 22, 1781, and Craig to Martin, September 29, 1781, Thomas Burke Papers Microfilm, Southern Historical Collection, University of North Carolina Library; *Royal Gazette* (New York), December 19, 1781, published by James Rivington. Hereafter cited as Rivington's *Royal Gazette.*

[28] Greene to Washington, October 25, 1781, in Sparks, *Correspondence of the American Revolution,* III, 431.

[29] Greene to Washington, November 21, 1781, Sparks, *Correspondence of the American Revolution,* III, 448; Greene to the President of Congress, October 25, 1781, Papers of the Continental Congress, no. 155, II, 361-363.

[30] Greene to the President of Congress, December 9, 1781, Papers of the Continental Congress, no. 155, II, 373-377, 378. The members of the committee were not named.

[31] Greene to Laurens, February 19, 1782, Nathanael Greene Papers, Henry E. Huntington Library and Art Gallery, San Marino, California.

[32] Ford and Hunt, eds., *Journals of the Continental Congress, 1774-1789,* XXI, 1073-1074. The garrisons of York and Gloucester were manned in part by Loyalists. Lieutenant Colonel Tench Tilghman, one of Washington's aides, carried Washington's dispatches of Cornwallis' surrender to Congress. On October 27, 1781, he wrote Washington that Congress was satisfied with the Articles of Capitulation except that the "So. Carolinians, whose animosities carry them to that length, that they think no treatment could have been too severe for the Garrison, the officers and Ld. Cornwallis in particular. One of them, whose name I will mention when I have the pleasure of meeting your Excellency, made

a motion that the officers should be detained until the further order of Congress." Burnett, *Letters of Members of the Continental Congress,* VI, 249.

[33] Washington to Greene, December 15, 1781, in John C. Fitzpatrick, ed., *The Writings of George Washington from the Original Manuscript Sources, 1745-1799,* (Washington: Government Printing Office, 1937), XXIII, 391.

[34] On April 12, 1782, Captain Joshua Huddy, a militia captain of artillery, was hanged by the "Associated Loyalists" under Captain Richard Lippincott. Washington on April 24 demanded in a letter to Clinton that Lippincott be turned over to him. In a series of events similar to those that followed Hayne's death, Washington sought and received on April 29 the approval of Congress to retaliate. On May 3 Washington directed that a captain who was an unconditional prisoner be chosen at random for retaliation. The man chosen, Captain Charles Asgill, was however covered under the stipulations of Cornwallis' surrender. A touchy situation erupted when delegates of Congress became interested in the case. When he heard that Lippincott was being held for court-martial for his participation in Huddy's death, Washington delayed the execution. Lippincott was later found not guilty on the grounds that he had been following orders of Governor William Franklin, commander of the Associated Loyalists. Washington was relieved of his difficult situation when Lady Asgill went to Paris and pleaded with Comte de Vergennes for her nineteen-year-old son's life. He in turn showed the plea to the king and queen, who interceded with Washington. Washington sent notice of this to Congress, who voted to release Asgill, an act Washington was only too glad to perform. See Henry Steele Commager and Richard B. Morris, eds., *The Spirit of 'Seventy-Six,* (New York: Bobbs-Merrill Co., Inc., 1958), II, 884-891; James Thomas Flexner, *George Washington in the American Revolution, 1775-1783,* (Boston: Little, Brown and Co., 1967), pp. 478-482; Douglas Southall Freeman, *George Washington, A Biography,* (New York: Charles Scribner's Sons, 1952), V, 412-425; Fitzpatrick, *The Writings of George Washington,* XXIV, 217-218; *Pennsylvania Packet,* May 2, May 9, May 21, and June 1, 1782; Rivington's *Royal Gazette,* May 18, 1782; *Royal Gazette* (Charlestown), June 6, 1782.

[35] Burke to Alexander Leslie, January 16, 1782, roll 4, frame 115, Thomas Burke Papers Microfilm. Lieutenant General Leslie was the new commander of British troops in the South and had held Burke prisoner.

[36] Burke to Jones, January 13, 1782, roll 3, frame 290; Burke to Leslie, January 18, 1782, roll 3, frame 291; Burke to Williams, March 28, 1782; Thomas Burke Papers Microfilm. Willie Jones was a senator from Halifax County, North Carolina; Colonel Williams was on Greene's staff.

[37] Rivington's *Royal Gazette,* March 13, 1782. On October 16, 1781, Baurmeister wrote of Rawdon: "Comte de Grasse was far nobler toward Lord Rawdon than Congress demanded; he refused to surrender him. His Lordship... will be sent directly to England as soon as they are paroled." Uhlendorf, trans., *Revolution in America,* p. 469.

[38] The following correspondence about Rawdon's exchange shows the delays involved. The exchange for Rawdon had begun late in December of 1781. Since Clinton held no French officers, he sent a list of American colonels he

would exchange for Rawdon to Comte de Rochambeau, commander of the French army. The exchange was delayed however in January. Rawdon had been paroled as a brigadier general and believed he could only be exchanged for another brigadier general, suggesting Moultrie. Moultrie was suitable to Clinton, but the American had already been exchanged. Clinton proposed Brigadier General Scott, who was captured in Charlestown in 1780. In June Rochambeau sent Rawdon's parole in exchange for Scott's. Rochambeau to Clinton, December 9, 1781; Clinton to Rochambeau, December 31, 1781; Rochambeau to Clinton, January 20, 1782; January 23, 1782; Clinton to Rochambeau, February 21, 1782; Rochambeau to Carleton, June 29, 1782, Great Britain, Historical Manuscripts Commission, *Report on American Manuscripts in the Royal Institute of Great Britain,* (London: Mackie and Co., 1906), 373, 383, 385, 402, 547. Hereafter cited as *Report on American Manuscripts.*

[39] *Royal Gazette* (Charlestown), August 18, 1781.

[40] John Bowman came from Scotland to America to look after his property and, although he had a pass, Balfour had imprisoned him. Bowman to Clinton, September 10, 1781-January 21, 1782, Henry Clinton Papers, William L. Clements Library, University of Michigan.

[41] Laurens to the Duke of Richmond, January 31, 1782, William Gilmore Simms Collection Microfilm, South Caroliniana Library.

[42] William Cobbett, *Cobbett's Parliamentary History of England, From the Earliest Period to the Year 1803,* (London: T.C. Hansard, 1814), XXII, 965-984; *Pennsylvania Packet,* May 7, 1782; *Historical Magazine,* X (September, 1866), 269-272.

[43] Leslie to Clinton, March 30, 1782, *Report on American Manuscripts,* II, 435-436.

[44] George Smith McCowen, Jr., *The British Occupation of Charleston, 1780-82,* (Columbia: University of South Carolina Press, 1972), p. 144.

[45] Greene to Leslie, February 1, 1782, *Report on American Manuscripts,* II, 391; see also Greene to Marion, January 28, 1782, in Gibbes, *Documentary History of the American Revolution,* III, 244.

[46] William Johnson, *Sketches of the Life and Correspondence of Nathanael Greene,* (Charleston: A.E. Miller, 1822), II, 196.

[47] William Gilmore Simms, *The Life of Nathanael Greene,* (New York: George F. Cooledge and Brother, 1849), p. 277.

[48] Franklin to Richard Oswald, July 28, 1782, in Francis Wharton, ed., *The Revolutionary Diplomatic Correspondence of the United States,* (Washington: Government Printing Office, 1889), V, 617-618. Oswald was appointed commissioner to make peace with the American colonies.

[49] Paine to Washington, September 7, 1782, in Sparks, *Correspondence of the American Revolution,* III, 533.

[50] Johnson, *Sketches of the Life and Correspondence of Nathanael Greene,* II, 196.

[51] William Edward Hayne to Jeremiah A. Yates, Charleston, December 23, 1835, William Edward Hayne Manuscript, South Caroliniana Library;

"Records Kept by Colonel Isaac Hayne," *South Carolina Historical and Genealogical Magazine,* XII (January, 1911), 14-23.

[52] Henry Laurens to the Duke of Richmond, January 31, 1782, William Gilmore Simms Collection Microfilm, South Caroliniana Library.

[53] Harden to Marion, April 18, 1781, in Gibbes, *Documentary History of The American Revolution,* III, 53-55; Letters Relating to Hayne, Library Company of Philadelphia.

[54] William Gilmore Simms, *The Partisan: A Romance of the Revolution,* (Chicago: Donohue, Henneberry and Co., 1890). John Shy indicates the frame of mind that enabled Hayne to make his decision to join the Patriots: "By 1780-1781, earlier in some places, most Americans, however weary, unhappy, or apathetic toward the rebellion they might be, were fairly sure of one thing: the British government no longer could or would maintain its presence, and sooner or later the rebels would return. Under these circumstances, civilian attitudes could no longer be manipulated by British policies or actions." John Shy, "The American Revolution: The Military Conflict Considered as a Revolutionary War," *Essays on the American Revolution,* Stephen G. Kurtz and James H. Hutson, eds., (New York: W.E. Norton and Co., Inc., 1973), p. 145.

Chapter Four
Epilogue: Patriot and Martyr

Contemporary accounts of Hayne's death reflected the indignation of Americans receiving the news. Generally the execution was looked upon as an illegal and irrational act committed at the whim of Colonel Balfour and Lord Rawdon.[1] The early accounts, often based on local legend and rumor, were written by men who were at times too close to the subject to be objective and whose interpretations were colored by a bias against Balfour and Rawdon. The early works mistook orders issued by Cornwallis for those issued by Clinton and confused the commands of Rawdon and Balfour.

A common thread running through the accounts is the portrayal of the execution as a vindictive act on the part of one or both of the British commanders. Dr. David Ramsay, a Patriot historian imprisoned at St. Augustine and later exiled to Philadelphia, described in 1785 the execution of his friend as a vengeful attempt on the part of Rawdon to revive his waning military fame after being "driven from almost the whole of his posts—baffled in all his schemes—and overwhelmed with vexation."[2]

In 1822 Alexander Garden compared the past records of Rawdon and Balfour. Executions in Camden, he noted, were not unusual under Rawdon's command, but no others were carried out in Charlestown under Balfour's administration. When an execution took place in Camden, the common question asked was not *who* was hanged but rather *how many*. Rawdon's order, "I will

Robert Y. Hayne (1791-1839), a cousin of Isaac Hayne, in 1828 attacked Lord Rawdon's letter defending his action in the Hayne affair. He held numerous public offices including United States senator and governor of South Carolina.

Paul Hamilton Hayne (1830-1886), cousin of Isaac Hayne and well-known Southern poet, edited *Russell's Magazine.* **in which William Gilmore Simms published "Hayne: A Dirge" in 1858.**

Isaac W. Hayne (1809-1880), grandson of Isaac Hayne, was attorney general of South Carolina. He wrote an article about his grandfather which appeared in the *Historical Magazine* **in 1867.**

give ten guineas for the head of any deserter belonging to the Volunteers of Ireland, and five guineas only, if he be brought alive," was given as proof of his severity.[3] Garden related the story—perhaps apocryphal—that Lieutenant Governor William Bull, who was carried, gravely ill, on a litter to Rawdon to plead for Hayne, later disclosed to a friend, "The unfortunate prisoner must die—I have used my best endeavors to save him, but Lord Rawdon is inexorable."[4] Garden, as Ramsay had before him, writing with the patriotic fervor of their times, viewed the execution as a calculated villainy on the part of Lord Rawdon.

A description that shows the contempt in which Balfour was held appeared in the 1802 history of the Revolution by General William Moultrie. He portrayed Balfour as a "proud, haughty Scot," who carried his "authority with a very harsh hand," and who had a "tyrannical, insolent disposition," and who treated "the people as the most abject slaves," even issuing an order "that every man who was not in his house by a certain day, should be subject to military execution."[5] The anonymous contemporary accounts of Hayne's death reported in the *New Jersey Gazette* on September 26 and October 10, 1781, share the belief that Hayne was ignominiously hanged by a mandate of Balfour.[6]

Colonel Henry Lee's memoirs, published in 1812, brought response from Lord Rawdon (by then Earl of Moira) in a lengthy letter dated June 24, 1813, at sea. Rawdon's letter was made public in Henry Lee, Junior's, *Campaign of 1781 in the Carolinas,* published in 1824.[7] Robert Y. Hayne, cousin of Isaac Hayne, answered Rawdon point for point in an article published in the *Southern Review* in 1828.[8]

The Hayne-Rawdon controversy probably accounts in part for James Stuart's remarks about his visit to Charleston in March of 1830. About the American Revolution in South Carolina he said, "One act of severity is, most of all, even to this day remembered,—the execution of Colonel Hayne, a citizen of Charleston, of great respectability of character, and large fortune." In his account of the events surrounding Hayne's death, Lord Rawdon is credited with ordering the execution. Stuart continued, "Lord Rawdon's cruelty while he commanded in South Carolina, is a theme of conversation even at the present day." He added, "Fortunately for

70

Lord Rawdon, afterwards Earl of Moira, and Marquis of Hastings, he lived long enough to establish a character for humanity and benevolence, founded on very different principles from those which influenced his conduct in early life in South Carolina."[9]

Isaac Hayne was, of course, seen differently from a Loyalist viewpoint. In that light he was seen as a "proper object" with whom to make an example. The Loyalist Thomas Jones felt that, if any man had been executed in revenge for Hayne, perhaps "an honest man of the greatest merit might have been sacrificed under pretence of appeasing the ghost of as great a villain, as infamous a traitor, and as perjured a scoundrel, as ever suffered under a gallows."[10] Another Loyalist, Alexander Chesney, an Irish immigrant, told of the capture of Hayne, who "deservedly suffered for treason."[11]

Hayne's fate was kept before the public when William Gilmore Simms began writing about the Revolution in South Carolina. The character Colonel Richard Walton in *The Partisan,* Simms' first Revolutionary novel, written in 1835, was based on Hayne. Simms also wrote about Hayne in his history of South Carolina in 1840, and his biographies of Francis Marion in 1844 and Nathanael Greene in 1849.[12] Hayne was also mentioned by Simms in a review article in *Simms' Monthly Magazine* or *The Southern and Western Monthly* of July, 1845. In it the story of Major André, the British officer executed as a spy, was told; the anguish felt at his death was compared to that felt later by the friends of Isaac Hayne.[13]

The character modeled after Hayne appeared again in 1850 with the serialized publication of Simms' *Katharine Walton* in *Godey's Magazine,* and in book form in 1851. This novel, which began where *The Partisan* left off, is a fictionalized version of Hayne's capture and execution. The book ascribed many of the events of Hayne's death to Colonel Walton. Balfour, who was cast as the villain, was described as "ignorant and self-opinionated," "feared and hated by his inferiors," "despised by his equals" and "utterly selfish." Simms continued his interest in Hayne by publishing a memorial to him called "Hayne: A Dirge" and by contributing a letter from Hayne's grandson Isaac W. Hayne to the *Historical Magazine.*[14]

In the early 1900s a book on Charleston gave an account of Hayne's death and said that "the ghostly effect produced on the popular mind by the tragic event was curiously shown by its giving rise to the only well-authenticated ghost story known in Charles Town." The story continued with details that Hayne had passed by the house of his sister-in-law on the way to the gallows and that a ghostly voice and the sound of footsteps could be heard in front of the house at night.[15]

Hayne was still being remembered in 1905 when his great-great grandson Franklin B. Hayne, a cotton merchant in New Orleans, expressed his concern over the "neglect of his ancestors by historians." He wrote, "If Isaac Hayne had been executed in Boston instead of Charleston, a monument would have been erected to him quite as high as the Bunker Hill monument, while in South Carolina no one even knows where he is buried."[16]

Twenty years later, Franklin Hayne was to receive the deed to the Hayne burial ground. He had visited the burial site and found that it was neglected. In response to a suggestion that the family erect a stone marker, he said that his "ancestor deserves more than a monument from one of his descendents. The nation furnished a monument to Nathan Hale, and his native state erected more than one in addition. I think my ancestor has much more right to be considered a 'Martyr of the Revolution' even than Nathan Hale, as great a patriot as he was. Therefore if this generation of South Carolinians do not see fit to honor his memory by erecting a monument, I do not care to do so but would rather have his tomb unnoticed, hoping that some future generation may consider it their duty to do what the last two generations have neglected."[17]

A resolution calling for the state to mark Hayne's grave was introduced in the South Carolina House of Representatives in 1929. On November 19 of that year a monument to Isaac Hayne, "Patriot and Martyr," was dedicated at his burial site near Jacksonborough.[18]

William Gilmore Simms captured the essence of Hayne's dilemma in his novel *The Partisan*. Colonel Walton (and Hayne) chose loyalty to family and property before any other considerations. A reviewer pointed out that Hayne's conflict was based "not so much from any want of patriotism, as from his entertaining too great a

The monument on the stone reads:

AS A GRATEFUL AND REVERENTIAL TRIBUTE
TO
A NOBLE MARTYR IN BEHALF OF LIBERTY
THE STATE OF
SOUTH CAROLINA
HAS ERECTED THIS MEMORIAL TO
COLONEL ISAAC HAYNE
WHO WAS CAPTURED NEAR HERE BY THE BRITISH
JULY 6, 1781 AND IN VIOLATION OF THE CUSTOMS
OF WAR WAS HANGED IN CHARLES TOWN AUGUST 4, 1781
AND WHOSE BODY WAS BURIED HERE IN HIS GARDEN
DULCE ET DECORUM EST PRO PATRIA MORI

HAYNE

Courtesy W.D. Workman, Jr.

The monument to Colonel Isaac Hayne in the Hayne Family Cemetery located near Jacksonboro, South Carolina.

73

love for domestic quietude, or perhaps from not at first sufficiently reflecting upon his duties to his country as a citizen and patriot."[19]

What this critic failed to realize—as did many of the early chroniclers of the Hayne affair—is that the participants in the drama were not bound by the rules of conventional warfare, where the parties involved were clearly on one side or the other. America's difficulty in combating guerrilla warfare over the last two decades in Indochina provides insight into the frustrations of Rawdon and Balfour as they tried in every way possible to secure the constantly shifting loyalties of the inhabitants.[20]

From this perspective we understand only too well the universal implications of the officer in the Southern army who described in 1782 the emotional state under which Hayne and his neighbors lived: "The people . . . have passed through a variety of changes and a choice of difficulties and misfortunes. The Human mind, perhaps owing to the fluctuating state of politics for the last two years, has undergone the most strange and [surprising?] revolutions that ever was known in any age or country."[21] This "fluctuating state of politics" among the British and the Americans triggered a series of events which culminated in the death of Isaac Hayne.

Footnotes, Chapter IV

[1] General P. Horry and M.L. Weems, *The Life of General Francis Marion,* (Philadelphia: Joseph Allen, 1839), pp. 204-211.

[2] David Ramsay, *The History of the Revolution of South-Carolina,* (Trenton: Isaac Collins, 1785), II, 250.

[3] Alexander Garden, *Anecdotes of the Revolutionary War in America,* (Charleston: A.E. Miller, 1822), pp. 255, 278. According to Franklin and Mary Wickwire this order was a ruse issued by Rawdon with the knowledge of the militia leaders to frighten their men. Franklin and Mary Wickwire, *Cornwallis: The American Adventure,* (Boston: Houghton Mifflin Co., 1970), p. 179.

[4] Alexander Garden, *Anecdotes of the American Revolution,* (Brooklyn: "The Union" Press, 1865), III, 173-174.

[5] William Moultrie, *Memoirs of the American Revolution, so Far as it Relates to the States of North and South Carolina and Georgia,* (New York: David Longworth, 1802), II, 252.

[6] Frank Moore, *Diary of the American Revolution from Newspapers and Original Documents,* (New York: Arno Press, 1969), II, 525.

[7] Henry Lee, *Memoirs of the War in the Southern Department of the United States,* (New York: University Publishing Co., 1869), pp. 613-620; Henry Lee, Jr., *Campaign of 1781 in the Carolinas,* (Philadelphia: E. Littell, 1824).

[8] Robert Y. Hayne, "The Execution of Colonel Isaac Hayne," *Southern Review,* I (1828), 70-106.

[9] James Stuart, *Three Years in North America,* (Edinburgh: Robert Cadell, 1833), II, 148-150.

[10] Both Edward de Lancey and Don Higginbotham quote from Roderick McKenzie that "Upon the entrance of General Greene into Carolina, Colonel Hayne accepted a commission in the American service in a secret manner. He came to Charleston, renewed his oaths of allegiance, and at his own request, was appointed to the command of a corps of militia. He remained long enough in the garrison to obtain every intelligence he wanted, and then went off with his regiment to the Americans; within two miles of Charleston he seized a number of sick and wounded British soldiers, and was guilty of some acts of barbarity." Thomas Jones, *History of New York during the Revolutionary War,* (New York:

Printed for the New York Historical Society, 1879), Edward Floyd de Lancey, ed., II, 214; Don Higginbotham, *The War of American Independence*, (New York: MacMillan Co., 1971), p. 362.

[11] Chesney went on saying Hayne had "communicated with the rebels while acting as a British commissary." Charles Cornwallis Chesney, *Essays in Military Biography*, (New York: Henry Holt and Co., 1874), pp. 336-337. I have no evidence to support this except that Hayne was selling produce from his plantation to the people in Charlestown, according to "America: Case of Col. Haynes," *The Scots Magazine*, XLIII (1782), 704.

[12] William Gilmore Simms, *The Partisan: A Romance of the Revolution; (Chicago: Donohue, Henneberry and Co., 1890)*; William Gilmore Simms, *The History of South Carolina*, (Charleston: Russell and Jones, 1860); William Gilmore Simms, *The Life of Francis Marion*, (New York: Derby and Jackson, (1858); William Gilmore Simms, *The Life of Nathanael Greene*, (New York: George F. Cooledge and Brother, 1849).

[13] "The Case of Major André—Miss Seward and Her Writings," *Southern and Western Monthly*, II (July, 1845), 33-41.

[14] William Gilmore Simms, *Katharine Walton: or the Rebel of Dorchester*, (Chicago: Donohue, Henneberry, and Co., 1890); "Hayne: A Dirge," *Russell's Magazine*, IV (December, 1858), 247-248. See Appendix I. Another poem in tribute to Hayne, "Death of Isaac Hayne," was written by Oliver Allstorm. Isaac Hayne Manuscripts, South Caroliniana Library. See Appendix II. *Historical Magazine*, 2nd ser., II (August, 1867), 76-78.

[15] Mrs. St. Julien Ravenel, *Charleston: The Place and the People*, (New York: MacMillan Co., 1906), p. 319.

[16] Hayne wrote to Theodore Jervey, who had prepared a genealogical article on the Hayne family for the *South Carolina Historical and Genealogical Magazine*. He added that he felt "very sore over the account of his death in Col. McCrady's 'History of South Carolina.' He gives a very good account of the circumstances leading up to his death, but winds up by saying he thinks the British were justified in hanging him. I can only say that Ramsay and all contemporary historians, considered the execution of Col. Isaac Hayne a stain on the British nation, and was not justified by the usages of war." Franklin B. Hayne to Theodore D. Jervey, June 3, 1905, Isaac Hayne Manuscripts, South Caroliniana Library.

[17] Franklin B. Hayne to Mrs. Jos. A. Bailey, May 22, 1926, Isaac Hayne Manuscripts, South Caroliniana Library. E.T.H. Shaffer of Walterboro had written a newspaper article, "A Little Journey to Hayne Hall." Franklin B. Hayne to E.T.H. Shaffer, March 12, 1926, Isaac Hayne Manuscripts, South Caroliniana Library. Mrs. N. Vaman Bailey wrote to Hayne concerning the erection of a government marker at Hayne's grave by the Daughters of the American Revolution. She felt the organization could put the marker up but that the family should erect a "stone worthy of his patriotism." N. Vaman Bailey to Franklin B. Hayne, May 12, 1926, Isaac Hayne Manuscripts, South Caroliniana Library.

[18] Margaret Hayne Harrison, *A Charleston Album*, (Rindge, New Hampshire: Richard R. Smith, Inc., 1953), p. 51. Beulah Glover. "He Showed His Enemies How to Die," *The State Magazine*, (August 3, 1952), p. 6. The ceremony was attended by an estimated five hundred people. President Hoover was among those sending telegrams.

[19] "The Partisan: A Tale of the Revolution," *Southern Literary Journal and Monthly Magazine*, I (January, 1836), 354.

[20] This is not to imply that the American Revolution and the Vietnam War are analogous. Rather I would concur with John Shy's observation: "We dare not argue that the American Revolutionary War was basically like modern revolutionary wars in Indochina and elsewhere; rather, we ask only whether the doctrines, the studies, and the general experience of 'revolutionary warfare' in the twentieth century provide some insight into the American Revolutionary War. The answer, with due caution and qualification, is yes." Johy Shy, "The American Revolution: The Military Conflict Considered as a Revolutionary War," *Essays on the American Revolution*, Stephen G. Kurtz and James H. Hutson, ed., (New York: W.W. Norton and Co., Inc., 1973), p. 123.

[21] *Pennsylvania Packet* (Philadelphia), April 6, 1782.

Appendix I

HAYNE: A DIRGE[1]

Let the death bell toll, for the parting soul,
It has paid for the pomp at a fearful price;
Spread gloom o'er the walls of your stately halls.
And deck your homes with each drear device;
For the city lies strangled by hostile power,
And the tyrant's foot is on temple and tower,
Yet one brave heart in that desolate hour,
Now makes himself ready for sacrifice!

II

And the toll of the bell, shall answer well,
As it lifts his soul o'er the tyrant's aim:
And well he knows, that the hate of foes,
Shall win from his people a deathless name;
He sees the black coffin his couch beside,
And the hangman cowers at his glance of pride,
While he walks his cell with a sovereign stride,
Since he feels that the morrow shall bring him fame.

III

With the morrow is Fame, but a death of shame,
A mortal agony first, and then,
A glad release to the realms of peace,

And a memory living 'mongst living men;
He hath led to the battle a noble band;
Hath fought the good fight for his father-land;
He hath won, he hath lost; but his battle brand
Shall flash in the eyes of his foes again!

IV

There are hands that shall wield, in the tented field,
The weapon so sacred in Freedom's sight;
And souls that shall rise, ere the martyr dies,
And pledge to his manes a deathless plight;
Never, while hostile foot shall tread,
The soil where the Sire has fought and bled,
To wreathe the good weapons whose flash hath shed,
For the cause of his people a glorious light!

V

There are friends who come in the hour of his doom,
Of gloom and of doom; but they have no fear;
But they cower, with their grief, for the noble chief,
Who answers their pleadings with words of cheer!
To the boy at his side, he says—"My son,
Be true to your country, for though but one,
You are one of a thousand, and realms are won,
Where a single great son shall in arms appear!"

VI

And the death-bells toll, for the parting soul,
And he walks 'mid the ranks of the marshall'd foe,
And he smiles as he sees that the balconies,
And windows have none who would see the show.
There is silence deep in each mansion proud,
Dread as deep, with no moaning loud,
But the citizen feels as the deathly shroud
Were wrapping himself in that common wo!

VII

Lo! the British are here, and the Hessians there,
And they form the square, round the scaffold high;
And the martyr comes, to the sound of drums,
And will show, by his death, how the brave should die,
He utters his prayer, that his God will spare,
But none to the Tyrant that's sovereign there;
And with brow erect, and soul above fear,
He dies for his country's liberty.

[1] William Gilmore Simms, "Hayne: A Dirge," *Russell's Magazine.* IV (December, 1858), 247-248.

Appendix II

DEATH OF ISAAC HAYNE[1]

When the British fought at Charleston
They captured Isaac Hayne,
And the British general thundered
"You have hope and much to gain,
If you swear your life's allegiance
To the Crown and to the King—
Or you'll never see your loved-ones
That's the verdict that we bring."

Hayne's dilemma was terrific,
For his wife and children three
Lay bedridden with the smallpox
While he fought for liberty.
So he struggled with his conscience
And agreed to their demand
On condition not to battle
Or bear arms against his land.

But the British broke their promise,
And commanded him to fight,
He refused, and with brave daring
Stole away one moonless night.
Then on reaching his militia,
Once again he struck, and lo—

Captured that base, turn-coat traitor
Andrew Williamson, the foe.

Loud the British cried for vengeance,
"Isaac Hayne—he must be got,
He must die upon the gallows
Ere our Williamson be shot."
So they searched in every forest
But their quest was all in vain;
For somehow, the British Red-Coats
Failed to capture Isaac Hayne.

Hayne fought on, his valor burning,
Independence was his goal!
To achieve it, he kept fighting
With the firebrand in his soul.
But his men were far outnumbered
By the clique that loved the Crown
So one sunset, they surprised him
And he laid his weapons down.

Once again he stood before them
Shackled and condemned to die
On the gallows ere the sunrise
Rose to brighten up the sky.
Once again he faced his judges
Firm, resigned, defiant still;
But his thoughts went flying homeward
To the loved-ones that were ill.

Then all Charleston prayed for mercy,
And his children knelt and cried,
For the wife and one dear daughter
Lay with others that had died.
But the Crown spurned all their pleadings
Hayne must suffer, Hayne must swing—
Just because he loved his country
More than any British king.

Thus our patriot and martyr
Died as martyrs always die;
Unafraid, for he saw freedom
Breaking through the darkened sky.
And his soul released from bondage
Now looks down upon the free—
Where the Stars and Stripes are waving
In the land of liberty!

[1] Oliver Allstorm, "Death of Isaac Hayne," Isaac Hayne Manuscripts, South Caroliniana Library.

Bibliography

I.   PRIMARY SOURCES, UNPUBLISHED
     A. Public Records
        Accounts Audited. South Carolina Archives.
        Charleston County Inventories. South Carolina Archives.
        Charleston County Wills. South Carolina Archives.
        Confiscated Estates MSS. South Carolina Archives.
        Jury and Tax Lists. South Carolina Archives.
        Subject File, Industry. South Carolina Archives.
        Treasury Journal and Ledgers. South Carolina Archives.
     B. Manuscripts
        British Headquarters (Sir Guy Carleton) Papers. Public
           Record Office Microfilm. South Carolina Archives.
        Thomas Burke Papers. Southern Historical Collection
           Microfilm. University of North Carolina Library.
        Cornwallis Papers. Public Record Office Microfilm. South
           Carolina Archives.
        Nathanael Greene Papers. Library of Congress Microfilm.
           South Carolina Archives.
        Nathanael Greene Papers. Henry E. Huntington Library and
           Art Gallery. San Marino, California.
        Letters Relating to Isaac Hayne. Manuscript Collection.
           Library Company of Philadelphia.
        Isaac Hayne MSS. South Caroliniana Library.
        William Edward Hayne MS. South Caroliniana Library.

Papers of the Continental Congress, 1774-1789. National Archives Microfilm. South Carolina Archives.

John Rutledge Letters. Charleston Library Society.

William Gilmore Simms Collection Microfilm. South Caroliniana Library.

George Washington Papers. Presidential Papers Microfilm. McKissick Library. University of South Carolina.

II. PRIMARY SOURCES, PUBLISHED

A. Newspapers

New-Hampshire Gazette and General Advertiser. Portsmouth, New Hampshire. 1781.

Pennsylvania Gazette and Weekly Advertiser. Philadelphia, Pennsylvania. 1781-1782.

Pennsylvania Packet or the General Advertiser. Philadelphia, Pennsylvania. 1781-1782.

Royal Gazette. Charleston, South Carolina. 1781-1782.

Royal Gazette. James Rivington, publisher. New York, New York. 1781-1782.

Royal Georgia Gazette. Savannah, Georgia. 1781.

Royal South-Carolina Gazette. Charleston, South Carolina. 1781-1782.

South Carolina and American General Gazette. Charleston, South Carolina. 1779.

Whitehall Evening-Post. London, England. 1781.

B. Periodicals

Annual Register. 1782.

Hibernian Magazine. 1782.

London Magazine or Gentleman's Monthly Intelligencer. 1782.

Scots Magazine. 1782.

C. Official Documents

Cobbett, William. *Cobbett's Parliamentary History of England. From the Earliest Period to the Year 1803.* 36 vols. London: 1806-20. Taken over by T.C. Hansard in 1812.

Cooper, Thomas, and David J. McCord. *The Statutes at Large of South Carolina.* 10 vols. Columbia: A.S. Johnston, 1838-1841.

Ford, Worthington C., and Gaillard Hunt, eds. *Journals of the Continental Congress, 1774-1789.* 34 vols. Washington: Government Printing Office, 1904-1937.

Hemphill, W.E., Wylma Anne Wates, and R. Nicholas Olsberg, eds. *Journals of the General Assembly and House of Representatives, 1776-1780.* Columbia: University of South Carolina Press, 1970.

"Journal of the Council of Safety," *Collections of the South Carolina Historical Society.* Vol. III. Charleston: South Carolina Historical Society, 1859.

Salley, A.S., ed. *Journal of the Senate of South Carolina, January 8, 1782-February 26, 1782.* Columbia: The State Company, 1941.

D. Private Papers and Miscellaneous Collections

Burnett, Edmund C., ed. *Letters of Members of the Continental Congress.* 8 vols. Washington: Carnegie Institution of Washington, 1921-1936.

Commager, Henry Steele, and Richard B. Morris, eds. *The Spirit of 'Seventy-Six.* 2 vols. New York: The Bobbs-Merrill Co., Inc., 1958.

Fitzpatrick, John C., ed. *The Writings of George Washington from the Original Manuscript Sources, 1745-1799.* 39 vols. Washington: Government Printing Office, 1931-1944.

Fortescue, John, ed. *The Correspondence of King George the Third, from 1760 to December 1783.* 6 vols. London: Frank Cass and Co., 1967.

Garden, Alexander. *Anecdotes of the American Revolution.* 3 vols. Brooklyn: "The Union" Press, 1865.

_____. *Anecdotes of the Revolutionary War in America.* Charleston: A.E. Miller, 1822.

Gibbes, Robert W. *Documentary History of the American Revolution.* 3 vols. New York: D. Appleton and Co., 1853-1857.

Great Britain. Historical Manuscripts Commission. *Report on American Manuscripts in the Royal Institution of Great Britain.* 4 vols. London: Mackie and Co., 1904-1909.

_____. Historical Manuscripts Commission. *Report on the Manuscripts of the Late Reginald Rawdon Hastings, Esq., of the Manor House, Ashby De La Zouch.* Edited by Francis Buckley. London: His Majesty's Stationary Office, 1934.

_____. Historical Manuscripts Commission. *Report on the Manuscripts of Mrs. Stopford-Sackville, of Drayton House, North Hamptonshire.* 2 vols. London: The Hereford Times, 1910.

Horry, Brig. Gen. P., and M.L. Weems. *The Life of General Francis Marion.* Philadelphia: Joseph Allen, 1839.

James, William Dobein. *A Sketch of the Life of Brigadier General Francis Marion.* Marietta, Georgia: Continental Book Company, 1948.

Johnson, William. *Sketches of the Life and Correspondence of Nathanael Greene.* 2 vols. Charleston: A.E. Miller, 1822.

Jones, E. Alfred, ed. *The Journal of Alexander Chesney, A South Carolina Loyalist in the Revolution and After.* Columbus, Ohio: Ohio State University, 1921.

Jones, Thomas. *History of New York during the Revolutionary War.* 2 vols. Edited by Edward Floyd de Lancey. New York: Printed for the New York Historical Society, 1879.

Lee, Henry. *Memoirs of the War in the Southern Department of the United States.* New York: University Publishing Co., 1869.

Lee, Henry, Jr. *Campaign of 1781 in the Carolinas.* Philadelphia: E. Littell, 1824.

Moore, Frank. *Diary of the American Revolution from Newspapers and Original Documents.* 2 vols. New York: Arno Press, 1969.

Moultrie, William. *Memoirs of the American Revolution.* 2 vols. New York: David Longworth, 1802.

Ramsay, David. *The History of the Revolution of South Carolina from a British Province to an Independent State.* 2 vols. Trenton: Isaac Collins, 1785.

Salley, A.S., Jr., ed. *Colonel William Hill's Memoirs of the Revolution.* Columbia: The State Company, 1921.

Sparks, Jared, ed. *Correspondence of the American Revolution: Being Letters of Eminent Men to George Washington.* 4 vols. Boston: Little, Brown, and Co., 1853.

Stedman, Charles. *The History of the Origin, Progress, and Termination of the American War.* 2 vols. Dublin: Messrs. P. Wogan, 1794.

Stevens, Benjamin Franklin, ed. *The Campaign in Virginia, 1781: An Exact Reprint of Six Rare Pamphlets on the Clinton-Cornwallis Controversy.* 2 vols. London: Charing Cross, 1888.

Stevens, Benjamin Franklin, ed. *Facsimiles of Manuscripts in European Archives Relating to America, 1773-1783.* 25 vols. Wilmington, Delaware: Mellifont Press, Inc., 1970.

Stuart, James. *Three Years in North America.* 2 vols. Edinburgh: Robert Cadell, 1833.

Tarleton, Banastre, *A History of the Campaigns of 1780 and 1781, in the Southern Provinces of North America.* London: T. Cadell, 1787.

Thacher, James. *Military Journal of the American Revolution.* Hartford: Hurlbut, Williams and Company, 1862.

Uhlendorf, Bernhard A., trans. *Revolution in America: Confidential Letters and Journals 1776-1784 of Adjutant General Major Baurmeister of the Hessian Forces.* New Brunswick: Rutgers University Press, 1957.

Walsh, Richard, ed. *The Writings of Christopher Gadsden, 1746-1805.* Columbia: University of South Carolina Press, 1966.

Wells, William Charles. *Two Essays: One upon Single Vision with Two Eyes; the other on Dew.* London: Printed for Archibald Constable and Co., Edinburgh, 1818.

Wharton, Francis, ed. *The Revolutionary Diplomatic Correspondence of the United States.* 6 vols. Washington: Government Printing Office, 1889.

Willcox, William B., ed. *The American Rebellion: Sir Henry Clinton's Narrative of His Campaigns, 1775-1785.* New Haven: Yale University Press, 1954.

Yearbook: City of Charleston, S.C., 1895. "Letters of the Honorable Richard Hutson." Charleston: Walker, Evans and Cogswell Co., 1895.

III. SECONDARY SOURCES

A. Books

Alden, John R. *The South in the Revolution, 1763-1789.* Baton Rouge: Louisiana State University Press, 1957.

Bancroft, George. *History of the United States of America, from the Discovery of the Continent.* 6 vols. New York: D. Appleton and Company, 1891.

Bass, Robert D. *Gamecock: The Life and Campaigns of General Thomas Sumter.* New York: Holt, Rinehart, and Winston, 1961.

_____ . *Swamp Fox: The Life and Campaigns of General Francis Marion.* London: Alvin Redman, 1960.

92

Boatner, Mark Mayo, III. *Encyclopedia of the American Revolution.* New York: David McKay Company, Inc., 1966.

Bótta, Charles. *History of the War of the Independence of the United States of America.* 2 vols. New Haven: Nathan Whiting, 1834.

Caldwell, Charles. *Memoirs of the Life and Campaigns of the Hon. Nathaniel Greene.* Philadelphia: J. Maxwell, 1819.

Carrington, Henry B. *Battles of the American Revolution, 1775-1781.* New York: A.S. Barnes and Co., 1876.

Chesney, Charles Cornwallis. *Essays in Military Biography.* New York: Henry Holt and Company, 1874.

Coleman, Kenneth. *The American Revolution in Georgia, 1763-1789.* Athens: University of Georgia Press, 1958.

Draper, Lyman C. *King's Mountain and Its Heroes.* Marietta, Georgia: Continental Book Company, 1954.

Faunt, Joan Schreiner Reynolds, Robert E. Rector, and David K. Bowden, comps. *Biographical Directory of the South Carolina House of Representatives.* Edited by Walter B. Edgar. Columbia: University of South Carolina Press, 1974.

Fisher, Sydney George. *The Struggle for American Independence.* 2 vols. Philadelphia: J.B. Lippincott Co., 1908.

Flexner, James Thomas. *George Washington in the American Revolution, 1775-1783.* Boston: Little, Brown and Co., 1967.

Fortescue, J.W. *A History of the British Army.* 13 vols. London: MacMillan and Co., 1899-1930.

Freeman, Douglas Southall. *George Washington: A Biography.* 7 vols. New York: Charles Scribner's Sons, 1948-1957.

Glover, Beulah. *Narrative of Colleton County: The Land Lying Between the Edisto and Combahee Rivers.* n.p., 1963.

Greene, George W. *Life of Nathanael Greene.* Boston: Charles C. Little and James Brown, 1848.

Gregorie, Anne King. *Thomas Sumter.* Columbia: R.L. Bryan Company, 1931.

Harrison, Margaret Hayne. *A Charleston Album.* Rindge, New Hampshire: Richard R. Smith, 1953.

Hennig, Helen Kohn. *Great South Carolinians From Colonial Days to the Confederate War.* Chapel Hill: University of North Carolina Press, 1940.

Higginbotham, Don. *The War of American Independence: Military Attitudes, Policies, and Practice, 1763-1789.* New York: The MacMillan Company, 1971.

Howe, George. *History of the Presbyterian Church in South Carolina.* 2 vols. Columbia: Duffie and Chapman, 1870.

Irving, Washington. *Life of George Washington.* 5 vols. New York: G.P. Putnam, 1860.

Johnson, Joseph. *Traditions and Reminiscences Chiefly of the American Revolution in the South.* Charleston: Walker and James, 1851.

Landrum, J.B.O. *Colonial and Revolutionary History of Upper South Carolina.* Greenville, S.C.: Shannon and Co., 1897.

Lossing, Benson J. *The Pictorial Field-Book of the Revolution.* 2 vols. Spartanburg: Reprint Co., 1969.

Lutnick, Solomon. *The American Revolution and the British Press, 1775-1783.* Columbia, Missouri: University of Missouri Press, 1967.

Malone, Dumas. *Dictionary of American Biography.* 20 vols. New York: Charles Scribner's Sons, 1932.

McCowen, George Smith, Jr. *The British Occupation of Charleston, 1780-82.* Columbia: University of South Carolina Press, 1972.

McCrady, Edward. *The History of South Carolina in the Revolution, 1775-1780.* New York: The MacMillan Company, 1901.

_____. *The History of South Carolina in the Revolution, 1780-1783*. New York: The MacMillan Company, 1902.

Metzger, Charles H. *The Prisoner in the American Revolution*. Chicago: Loyola University Press, 1971.

Mills, Robert. *Statistics of South Carolina*. Charleston: Hurlbut and Lloyd, 1826.

Peckham, Howard H. *The War for Independence: A Military History*. Chicago: University of Chicago Press, 1958.

Rankin, Hugh F. *Francis Marion: The Swamp Fox*. New York: Thomas Y. Crowell Company, 1973.

Ravenel, Mrs. St. Julien. *Charleston: The Place and the People*. New York: The MacMillan Company, 1906.

Reynolds, Emily Bellinger, and Joan Reynolds Faunt. *Biographical Directory of the Senate of the State of South Carolina, 1776-1964*. Columbia: South Carolina Archives, 1964.

Sabine, Lorenzo. *Biographical Sketches of Loyalists of the American Revolution with an Historical Essay*. 2 vols. Boston: Little, Brown, and Co., 1864.

Schenck, David. *North Carolina, 1780-81*. Raleigh, North Carolina: Edward and Broughton, 1889.

Simms, William Gilmore. *The History of South Carolina*. Charleston: Russell and Jones, 1860.

_____. *Katharine Walton: or the Rebel of Dorchester*. Chicago: Donohue, Henneberry and Co., 1890.

_____. *The Life of Francis Marion*. New York: Derby and Jackson, 1858.

_____. *The Life of Nathanael Greene*. New York: George F. Cooledge and Brother, 1849.

_____. *The Partisan: A Romance of the Revolution*. Chicago: Donohue, Henneberry and Co., 1890.

_____. *South-Carolina in the Revolutionary War*. Walker and James, 1853.

Snowden, Yates. *History of South Carolina.* 5 vols. Chicago: The Lewis Publishing Co., 1920.

Stephen, Leslie, and Sidney Lee, eds. *Dictionary of National Biography.* 22 vols. London: Oxford University Press, 1949-1950.

Stevens, William Oliver. *Charleston: Historic City of Gardens.* New York: Dodd, Mead and Company, 1939.

Thayer, Theodore G. *Nathanael Greene: Strategist of the American Revolution.* New York: Twayne, 1960.

Treacy, M.F. *Prelude to Yorktown: The Southern Campaign of Nathanael Greene, 1780-1781.* Chapel Hill: University of North Carolina Press, 1963.

Van Doren, Carl. *Secret History of the American Revolution.* New York: The Viking Press, 1951.

Wallace, David D. *The History of South Carolina.* 4 vols. New York: The American Historical Society, Inc., 1934.

_____. *South Carolina: A Short History, 1520-1948.* Columbia: University of South Carolina Press, 1969.

Wallace, Willard M. *Appeal to Arms: A Military History of the American Revolution.* New York: Harper and Brothers, 1951.

Ward, Christopher. *The War of the Revolution.* Edited by John R. Alden. 2 vols. New York: MacMillan and Co., 1952.

Weigley, Russell F. *The Partisan War: The South Carolina Campaign of 1780-1782.* Columbia: University of South Carolina Press, 1970.

Wickwire, Franklin, and Mary B. *Cornwallis: The American Adventure.* Boston: Houghton Mifflin Company, 1970.

B. Articles

Hayne, Isaac. "Records Kept by Colonel Isaac Hayne." *South Carolina Historical and Genealogical Magazine,* X (July, 1909), 145-170.

Hayne, Isaac W. "Colonel Isaac Hayne." *Historical Magazine,* 2nd Ser., II (August, 1867), 76-78.

Hayne, Robert Y. "The Execution of Colonel Isaac Hayne." *Southern Review,* I (1828), 70-106.

Jervey, Theodore D. "The Hayne Family." *South Carolina Historical and Genealogical Magazine,* V (July, 1904), 168-188.

"Lord Rawdon and the Duke of Richmond, on the Execution of Colonel Isaac Hayne." *Historical Magazine,* X (September, 1866), 269-272.

"The Partisan: A Tale of the Revolution." *Southern Literary Journal and Monthly Magazine,* I (January, 1836), 347-358.

Salley, A.S., Jr. "Capt. John Colcock and Some of his Descendents." *South Carolina Historical and Genealogical Magazine,* III (1902), 216-241.

Shy, John. "The American Revolution: The Military Conflict Considered as a Revolutionary War." *Essays on the American Revolution.* Edited by Stephen G. Kurtz and James H. Hutson. New York: W.W. Norton and Co., Inc., 1973.

Simms, William Gilmore. "The Case of Major Andre— Miss Seward and Her Writings." *Southern and Western Monthly,* II (July, 1845), 33-41.

_____ . "Hayne: A Dirge." *Russell's Magazine,* IV (December, 1858), 247-248.

C. Unpublished Thesis

Farrior, John Edward. "The Use of Historical Characters by William Gilmore Simms in His Romances of the Revolution." Unpublished M.A. Thesis, University of North Carolina, 1944.

Index

Aera Ironworks, 16, 22n
André, John, 30, 36, 71; silhouette of, 37
Arnold, Benedict, 36
Asgill, Charles, 58, 64n
Asgill, Lady, 64n
Augusta, Ga., 18, 26, 28, 39
Bailey, N. Vaman, 76n
Balfour, Nisbet, 13, 26, 27, 29, 30, 31, 32, 35, 36, 38, 39, 42n, 43n, 44n, 45n, 47, 49, 50, 52, 55, 56, 57, 58, 59, 61n, 65n, 67, 70, 71, 74
Ballingall, Robert, 20
Barry, Maj., 44n
Bath, Eng., 57
Baurmeister, Carl Leopold, 63n
Beaufort, S.C., 16
Board of Police, 20, 32
Boston, Mass., 72
Boudinot, Elias, 54
Bowman, John, 57, 65n
Brandywine, Pa., battle of, 36
Brest, Fr., 56
Brooklyn, N.Y., battle of, 36
Brown, Thomas, 27, 39
Buford, Abraham, 18
Bunker's Hill, Mass., battle of, 35, 36, 45n
Bull, William, 32, 44n, 70
Burke, Thomas, 53, 56, 64n
Camden, S.C., 18, 25, 26, 35, 38, 39, 41n, 46n, 67
Carleton, Sir Guy, 65n
Cattell, B., 63n
Charlestown, S.C. (after 1783, Charleston), 11, 15, 16, 17, 18, 20, 23n, 25, 26, 27, 29, 30, 31, 32, 33, 35, 36, 42n, 45n, 47, 49, 53, 54, 56, 57, 61n, 65n, 70, 72, 75n, 76n, 83, 84
Charlotte, N.C., 25
Cheraw, S.C., 25
Chesney, Alexander, 71, 76n
Churches: Bethel Presbyterian, 15; Stoney Creek, 15; Independent, 15

Clinton, Sir Henry, 18, 23n, 26, 27, 28, 29, 43n, 57, 58, 64n, 65n, 67
Colcock, John, 31, 34
Colleton Co., S.C., 15
Congaree River, 42n, 50
Continental Congress, 11, 32, 47, 49, 50, 51, 52, 53, 54, 58, 63n, 64n, 65n
Cornwallis, Lord Charles (Earl and Marquis), 11, 25, 26, 27, 30, 35, 36, 39, 41n, 42n, 46n, 50, 52, 53, 54, 56, 64n, 67; portrait of, 55
Cowpens, S.C., battle of, 26
Craig, James, 53
Cruger, J. Harris, 27, 28, 38, 41n
Deane, Mary; see Hayne, Mary (Deane)
Dickinson, John, 42n, 43n
Dorchester, S.C., 16, 27
Elizabethtown, N.J., battle of, 36
England, 27, 35, 45n, 53, 57, 65n
Eutaw Springs, S.C., battle of, 53
Exchange Building, 30, 33
Execution, 11, 13, 15, 31, 32, 33, 34, 35, 39, 44, 46n, 48, 49, 51, 52, 53, 54, 55, 56, 58, 59, 61n, 64n, 67, 68, 69, 70, 71, 72, 76n
Fenwick, Col., 42
Ferguson, Patrick, 25
Ferguson, Thomas, 63n
Fishing Creek, S.C., battle of, 25
Fort Balfour, 42n
Fort Granby, 26
Fort Motte, 26
Fort Moultrie, 18
Fortesque, J.W., 19, 45n
Franklin, Benjamin, 58
Franklin, William, 64n
Fraser, Charles, 30, 32
Fraser, Thomas, 29, 51, 61n
Friday's Ferry, 27
Gadsden, Christopher, 53
Garden, Alexander, 67, 70
Gates, Horatio, 25, 39

Georgetown, S.C., 27, 41n
Georgia, 16
Germain, Lord George, 28
Germantown, Pa., battle of, 36
Godey's Magazine, 71
Grasse, Comte de, 56, 57, 65n
Greene, Nathanael, 11, 25-27, 29, 30,
    32, 39, 41n, 43n, 63n, 71, 75n; faced
    with retaliating for Hayne's death,
    49; portrait of, 48; proclamation
    threatening retaliation, 50, 51-52,
    62n; question of retaliation, 53, 54,
    56, 58, 59
Guilford Courthouse, N.C., battle of,
    26

Hale, Nathan, 13, 72
Halifax Co., N.C., 64n
Harden, William, 27, 28, 29, 42n, 47,
    49, 50, 51, 59
Harleston, Isaac, 43n
Hayne, Eliza, 24n
Hayne, Elizabeth (1774-   ), 16
Hayne, Elizabeth (Hutson), 15, 16, 24n
Hayne, Franklin B., 72, 76n
Hayne, Isaac (1714-1751), 15; will of,
    21n
Hayne, Isaac (1745-1781), frontispiece,
    11, 12, 13, 18, 20, 22n, 23n, 24n, 28,
    36, 39, 42n, 43n, 44n, 45n, 47, 48, 49,
    51, 52, 53, 54, 55, 56, 57, 58, 59, 61n,
    64n, 66n, 68, 69, 70, 74, 75n, 76n;
    birth, 15; early life, 15, 16; takes
    oath of allegiance, 20; becomes
    colonel in S.C. militia, 29; captures
    Andrew Williamson, 29; taken
    prisoner, 29; held prisoner, 30;
    sentenced to death, 31; granted stay
    of execution, 32; painting of Hayne
    being led to his execution, 33;
    accounts of his death, 32, 34; threat
    of retaliation for death of, 50; con-
    temporary accounts of, 71; ghost of,
    72; monument to, 72, 73; poems
    about, 79-81, 83-85
Hayne, Isaac (1766-1802), 16, 44n

Hayne, Isaac W. (1809-1880), portrait
    of, 69; 71
Hayne, John (d. c. 1718), 15
Hayne, John (1773-1825), 16
Hayne, Mary (1768-1768), 16
Hayne, Mary (1776-1780), 16, 24n
Hayne, Mary (Deane), 15
Hayne, Paul Hamilton, portrait of, 69
Hayne, Robert Y., 16, 24n, 70; portrait
    of, 68
Hayne, Sarah (1770-1800), 16, 44n
Hayne, Sarah (Williamson), 15
Hayne, William Edward, 16, 24n, 32,
    44n
Hayne family cemetery, monument to
    Isaac Hayne, 73
Hayne family coat of arms, 17
Hessians, 45n, 83
Higginbotham, Don, 75n
High Hills of Santee, 27, 49
Hill, William, 16, 22n
Hillsborough, N.C., 53
Historical Magazine, 69, 71
Hobkirk's Hill, S.C., battle of, 26
Hoover, Herbert, 77n
House of Lords, 11, 57
Huddy, Joshua, 56, 58, 64n
Huntington, Lord, 56, 57
Hutson, Elizabeth; **see** Hayne,
    Elizabeth (Hutson)
Hutson, Richard, 16, 18, 22n, 23n, 63n
Hutson, William, 15
India, 19
Indochina, 74, 77n
Ireland, 27, 41n

Jacksonborough, S.C., 16, 72, 73
James Island, S.C., 56
Jarvis, Mr., 30
Johnson, William, 39
Jones, Thomas, 71
Jones, Willie, 64n
Katharine Walton, 71
King's Mountain, S.C., battle of, 25, 36
Ladson, Capt., 23n
Ladson, James, 43n
Lafayette, Marquis de, 62n

Lancey, Edward de, 75n
Laurens, Henry, 57
Laurens, John, 54
Lee, Henry, 26, 27, 36, 41n, 50, 67
Lee, Henry, Jr., 70
Leigh, Sir Egerton, 32, 44n
Leslie, Alexander, 57, 58, 64n
Lexington, Mass., 35
Lincoln, Benjamin, 25
Lippincott, Richard, 64n
London, Eng., 28
Long Island, N.Y., battle of 35, 36
Loyalists, 22n, 23n, 25, 28, 30, 32, 39,
    44n, 49, 51, 53, 56, 57, 61n, 63n, 64n,
    71
McCrady, Edward, 30, 46n, 76n
McKenzie, Roderick, 75n
McLoughlan, Lt. Col., 29
McQueen, John, 43n
Marion, Francis, 26, 27, 28, 41n, 42n,
    47, 49, 51, 71
Martin Alexander, 53
Mathews, John, 51
Middleton, Arthur, 54
Militia, 13, 15, 16, 20, 27, 28, 34, 38, 39,
    47, 49, 51, 54, 59, 62n, 83; Colleton
    Co. Regiment of, 18, 23n, 29, 42n
Monck's Corner, S.C., 26, 27
Monmouth, N.J., battle of, 35
Morgan, Daniel, 25, 26
Motte, Isaac, 54
Moultrie, William, 38, 39, 65n, 70
Nelson's Ferry, S.C., 41n
Neufville, Isaac, 32, 44n
New Acquisition, S.C., 16
New Jersey, 54, 58
New Jersey Gazette, 70
New Orleans, La., 72
New York, 25, 35, 36, 57, 58
Ninety Six, S.C., 18, 27, 28, 30, 36, 38,
    41n, 46n
North Carolina, 25, 26, 53, 56
Oaths of Allegiance, 18, 20, 24n, 35,
    46n, 59, 75n
Orangeburg, S.C., 26, 27, 30
Orphan House Building, 45n

Oswald, Richard, 66n
Paine, Thomas, 58
Paris, Fr., 64n
Parishes: St. Bartholomew's, 15, 16; St.
    Paul's, 16, 22n
Paroles, 18, 20, 23n, 34, 39, 57
Partisan, The, 59, 71, 72
Patriots, 35, 36, 38, 49, 51, 58, 66n
Patterson, James, 20, 36
Peronneau, Aunt, 44n
Philadelphia, Pa., 67
Pickens, Andrew, 26, 27, 59
Pinckney, Col., 43n
Plantations: Hayne Hall, 16; Pear Hill,
    16; Sycamore, 16
Pocotaligo, S.C., 42n
Pon Pon, S.C., 15, 29, 42n
Powell, Robert William, 32, 44n
Pringle, Mssrs., 43n
Prison ships, 20, 49
Prisoners, 18, 20, 24n, 29, 32, 35, 39,
    42n, 49, 50, 51, 53, 62n, 64n, 65n, 70
Proclamations, 18, 23n, 27, 28, 35, 46n,
    50, 51, 58, 62n
Provost Prison, 31
Purisburg, S.C., 42n
Radcliffe's Garden, 44n
Ramsay, David, 46n, 63n, 67, 76n
Rawdon, Lord Francis (Earl of Moira
    and Marquis of Hastings), 13, 18,
    23n, 26, 27, 30, 31, 32, 35, 36, 38, 39,
    41n, 42n, 43n, 44n, 45n, 47, 52, 53,
    56, 57, 58, 59, 65n, 67, 68, 70, 71, 74,
    75n; portrait of, 19
Reid, James, 16
Retaliation, 11, 48, 49, 50, 51, 52, 53,
    54, 56, 58, 59, 63n, 64n
Richmond, Duke of, 11, 57
Rochambeau, Comte de, 65n
Royal Gazette, 15, 45n, 47
Rugely, Henry, 38
Russell's Magazine, 69
Rutledge, John, 20, 39, 42n, 43n, 47, 49,
    50, 51, 61n
St. Augustine, Fla., 49, 50, 67
Santee River, 41n, 42n

Savannah, Ga., 28
Scotland, 65n
Scott, Brig. Gen., 65n
Scott, John, 43n
Shropshire, Eng., 15
Shy, John, 66n, 77n
Simmons' Island, S.C., 18, 23n
Simms' Monthly Magazine, 71
Simms, William Gilmore, 44n, 59, 69, 71, 72
Simpson, James, 20, 32
Smallwood, William, 39
Sons of Liberty, 39
South Carolina, 15, 19, 22n, 25, 26, 28, 31, 34, 36, 47, 51, 53, 54, 59, 70, 71, 72
Southern and Western Monthly, The: see *Simms' Monthly Magazine*
Southern Review, 70
Stafford Co., Va., 63n
Staten Island, N.Y., 36
Stewart, Alexander, 27, 42n
Stuart, James, 70
Sumter, Thomas, 25, 26, 27
Tarleton, Banastre, 25, 26
Tilghman, Tench, 63n
Tories; see Loyalists

Tower of London, 57
Vergennes, Comte de, 64n
Vietnam War, 77n
Virginia, 26
Volunteers of Ireland, 70
Walton, Richard, 59, 71, 72
Washington, George, 38, 50, 53, 54, 58, 63n, 64n; thoughts about retaliation, 56
Washington, William, 53, 63n
Watson, Lt. Col., 41
Waxhaws, S.C., 18
Wells, Robert, 45n
Wells, William Charles, 35, 45n
West Point, N.Y., 36
Whigs; see Patriots
Williams, Col., 64n
Williamson, Andrew, 29, 34, 42n, 43n, 84
Williamson, Sarah; see Hayne, Sarah (Williamson)
Wilmington, N.C., 26, 53
Winnsborough, S.C., 25
Wright, Alexander, 32, 44n
Wright's Bluff, S.C., 41n
Yates, Jeremiah, 44n
Yorktown, Va., battle of, 11, 13, 53, 56

David K. Bowden

is a Ph.D. candidate and teaching associate in the History Department of the University of South Carolina. As a holder of the Joan Schreiner Reynolds Faunt Memorial Fellowship, Bowden was one of the compilers of the **Biographical Directory of the South Carolina House of Representatives.** While at the University, he has been the recipient of both the Region III and District 8 Colonial Dames Scholarships for work in South Carolina history and the Lilly Endowment Fellowship for research on South Carolina in the Revolution.

A writer of articles on the American Revolution, he contributed to **South Carolina in Revolution**, the Bicentennial Edition of **The State** newspaper. While serving on the Richland County Bicentennial Advisory Committee, he was a contributing writer to its publication, **The Spirit of the Times.** He also will be the author of a sketch in **The Dictionary of North Carolina Biography.**

Bowden delivered a paper at the recent conference on William Gilmore Simms and the Revolution in South Carolina, held at the College of Charleston. The proceedings of the conference will be published by the Southern Studies Program at the University of South Carolina. In connection with Southern Studies and the South Carolina Commission for the Humanities, he has been a visiting lecturer on South Carolina figures in the American Revolution.

Presently Bowden is writing his dissertation, "The South and the American Army, 1848-1860," and teaching American history at the University of South Carolina.